John Vonhof

The Alban Guide to Managing the Pastoral Search Process

An Alban Institute Publication

Library of Congress Catalog Card Number 99-72203

ISBN 1-56699-213-3

This book is dedicated to pastoral search committees and pastors.

CONTENTS

PREFACE

A story is told of a pastor answering the telephone one evening to be greeted by an elder from another church wanting to ask him a question. The elder asked, "Our church is searching for a new pastor and I was wondering if you are open to a call?" When the pastor indicated that he did not wish to consider a call since he had only been at his church for three years, he heard a loudly audible, "Oh shoot!" from the elder. "Are you sure?" the elder asked, "I need to come up with three names by tomorrow!" Another pastor tells of not knowing he was under consideration by a certain church until he was asked whether he would consider their call!

One pastor reported that after having lunch with a search committee, the committee members began to split up the check, and the pastor almost had to pay for his own lunch. At least the committee had joined him for lunch. During a break between meetings, another candidate ate dinner alone after he was given a voucher for a local restaurant and was told, "You can walk there!"

Imagine the surprise of a candidate when she received a letter telling her the date and time of her interview. No one had bothered to ask about her schedule! And finally, after driving two hours for an evening meeting, another candidate was not shown where the bathroom was, not offered a cup of coffee, and no one offered to hang up her coat.

Such can be the experiences pastors have with some search committees. It is this style of approach and callousness that all search committees should avoid. The examples above are not uncommon, because many pastoral search committees operate in the unknown. Many churches have not had to manage a pastoral search process for 10, 15, or even 20 years. Search committee members, from board members to the actively involved lay member, do not typically understand the multitude of tasks that make up the search process. Much of the resource material available to search committees addresses the issues in generalities and does not begin to identify the specific tasks or how to manage them.

Could your board and church begin the search process if your pastor announced today that he or she had accepted a call and would be leaving in three weeks? Could you manage the pastoral search process with the quality effort it deserves? These are only two of the many complicated questions that face pastoral search committees at any given time. To further complicate the process, the pool of available pastors is generally not large enough to satisfy the demand. What are search committees to do?

The pastoral search committee has a complex task before it. In order to have a clear focus, its process must be well thought out and free from unnecessary distractions. This book is aimed at detailing the process in enough depth for church boards to understand how to form a search committee and then to help the newly formed committee understand the strategy and the order of the multitude of tasks before it. With a clear understanding of the process, all will realize that the search process cannot be hurried.

Serving on a pastoral search committee requires a deep commitment to the Lord and the local church. Much time and energy will be required before the task is completed. The process will likely take a minimum of six months and as long as two years. The way the search process is managed can make a difference in your finding a good pastoral match, in shortening the length of the search effort, and in reducing the stress on all parties involved. Whether your church is in a metropolitan area or rurally located; or whether yours is the only local church of your denomination, or one of many congregations from the same denomination, or an independent, you must manage the search process with high standards of excellence. You are not allowed the luxury of sitting back, putting out a few ads, sending out a handful of letters, and then waiting for pastors to beat down your church door wanting to serve as your pastor. You need to conduct an intentional, high quality search that treats pastors, and the process, with respect.

You need to be competitive and thorough in your efforts. You may not think that the words *competitive* or *compete* are appropriate when talking about the pastoral search process, yet consider that when one church becomes vacant, it simply becomes one more in a large circle of vacant churches. Each of these congregations is working to find a pastor with the right ministry skills to best match its gifts and needs. Each is using the best resources it can develop to present its church in the best light possible. Several may ultimately issue calls to the same pastor. Whether or not you like the words, the process is competitive and churches do compete for pastors. Search committees do not need to focus on this aspect of the process, but they should be aware of it. Each church enters into the search process with its own unique set of strengths and needs, and the pastors it considers have their own special ministry gifts and skills. The search process should result in creating the best match for both the pastor and the church.

This book is designed to allow individuals with little or no experience to serve effectively as members of a pastoral search committee. All committee members should read through this book at least once. While it provides detailed information to the committee chairperson, it also offers committee members a general overview of how the process is managed and why. The full committee will then understand what its task is and how it can conduct a quality search.

Each search committee may use or modify the information presented, or it may skip over information that does not apply to its situation. The examples of letters, surveys, and questionnaires are given for you to build on, not simply to copy. Make these examples your own. Work with them. By adding and subtracting data and by making them into a format that you are comfortable with, you will create your own personalized style of search, materials, and correspondence.

Throughout the manual are many charts called task clusters. These charts illustrate the flow of tasks that typically happen during a search process. By following the arrows of the activities in these clusters, the search committee will be helped to think through the steps it needs to consider and see them in a broader context. Review these task clusters after reading the chapter in which they are found and refer back to them as you work step-by-step through the search process.

As the search committee manages the search process, it must adhere to denominational and regional requirements. It is the responsibility of the church board and the supervisor, counselor, or other denominational liaison to help the search committee understand these requirements. However, this does not relieve the search committee from the responsibility of also understanding them.

Recognizing that many churches ordain women as pastors, the text refers to both male and female pastors. Names of people, churches, and cities used in this book are fictitious.

This book was born in pastoral search committee meetings. As we struggled with the process, we learned much about what we did not want to do and much about what we needed to do to be effective. We also often found ourselves in an undefined process in which we were on our own to choose what we did, how we did it, and in what order we did it. During our search I realized that there was a need for a book about managing the pastoral search process. While written for managing a pastoral search, this book can also serve a search committee that is looking for other staff members.

My prayers are with you as you seek God's will in your search for your next pastor.

I want to thank several people who read all or parts of this manuscript and gave suggestions and encouragement. They include Cheryl Cooper, Gary Dalman, Marion Pryfogle, Kent Roberts, Daniel Sevenson, and Dennis Shirron. The search committee of Christ's Community Church in Hayward, California, provided the inspiration to write about what we learned. My wife Kathie offered a patient and supporting ministry as a sounding board for ideas. Beth Ann Gaede of the Alban Institute was a joy to work with as she provided a wealth of positive feedback and constructive criticism that brought clarity to the manuscript. The Lord brought these individuals into my life at the right time to bless this work. Thank you Lord.

CHAPTER 1

The Pastoral Search Committee

Pastors' Perspectives

A survey of pastors indicates that every search process has room for improvement. The survey posed questions about the process, the picture the search committee presented, factors that influenced their decisions, and things the search committee could have done better. Consider the following candid statements by pastors regarding the search processes they have experienced. Use their comments to help your search committee conduct a high-quality search.

- "The secretary did all the legwork, which resulted in an effort to call 'his kind of man' who, as it turned out, I was not."
- "I respected those making an effort to find a match for their vision more than those simply scrambling to fill the position."
- "Search committees should focus much more effort on the issues of leadership and followership, such as seeking a pastor who is a leader and preparing their people for following."
- "Their search effort was poorly managed."
- "A search committee member who is enthusiastic about his or her church is hard to say 'No' to."

Beginning the Search Process

If your denomination does not have guidelines about beginning a search, the question of when to begin the search process may be open for debate.

Pastors would often prefer the process to begin after they leave. They may feel the questions and surveys can wait. Some pastors indicate that to begin the search process before they leave does not allow proper closure for them, their families, and for their congregations. On the other hand, the board is concerned about the upcoming vacancy and would like to have the process under control. Realizing that the position may be vacant for anywhere from nine months to two years, boards will often feel they must move quickly to form a search committee and get the process moving. Deciding when to start the process (and whether to conduct a congregational survey or ask for congregational input before the current pastor leaves) may be jointly decided by the board and the search committee.

When to start may also be based on whether or not the existing pastor will be involved in the formation of the search committee. Some pastors are comfortable helping; others are not. Some denominations have rules about involvement by the outgoing pastor. The decision may also be based on the relationship between pastor and board, and between pastor and congregation. Talk candidly to your pastor. The decision on when to begin the search process is ultimately up to the board or the search committee. Do not compromise either the formation of the committee or their start-up activities.

Formation of the Pastoral Search Committee

The pastoral search committee, or call committee as it may also be called, has a tremendously complex task, but one that can bring many rewards. Before discussing the search committee membership, consider several important perspectives about the committee. Members of a search committee are given the task of discovering the person God would have pastor their church. It could be said that your committee needs individuals with a combination of both "head smart" and "heart feeling." For that reason, committee members should rank high in four areas: spiritual sensitivity, ability to work well in a committee setting, listening and communication skills, and ability to take an active role in the ministries of the church. They should also understand the church's vision and mission. Although search committee members will be at different levels in the four areas, they must all have an enthusiasm for their task. It is this enthusiasm that will carry them forward through the long process ahead.

Whether the search committee is chosen by the board or selected by a nominating committee or the congregation, the same considerations need to be given to committee leadership, congregational representation, and size.

Search Committee Leadership

The search committee needs a strong leader to serve as chairperson. This person should be comfortable leading in a committee setting; have gifts and skills in organizing, administrating, providing encouragement, and stating consensus; and be comfortable speaking to groups. Strong clerical support is also needed. The amount of paperwork generated by and tracked by a secretary can be overwhelming to an individual unfamiliar with handling agendas, minutes, letters, and phone calls to multiple people–all at the same time. In choosing members for the committee, the board should decide whether it will select whom it wants to serve as chairperson and secretary and approach these two individuals on a one-to-one basis, or whether it will ask the members of the search committee to choose these officers amongst themselves. There may be occasions when the chairperson and secretary share duties, and this approach may be useful if people have qualms either about their ability to serve or the time it will require. If you have rules in your bylaws or denominational policies about who may serve in these positions, follow those guidelines.

Congregational Representation

It is crucial for the search committee to be made up of a cross section of the membership of the congregation. As you consider individuals, think about who can represent your congregation's various constituencies. A good balance of gender and age is positive. You should not, however, compromise having qualified members who fit the four areas above simply to have all cross sections represented. Try to have at least one member who is also on the church board. This person should represent the board to the search committee and the search committee back to the board. The committee does not have to be large. Eight members is optimum. Some churches base the size of the committee on the size of the congregation. As you consider committee size, remember the pros and cons of the different sizes.

With more than eight on a search committee:

- *Pros*: You may gain a larger cross section of the congregation, with more skilled people to share in the tasks of an effective search.
- *Cons*: Discussions, conference calls, and decision making become more difficult to manage, and the meetings will have to be very structured and may last longer.

With eight or fewer on a search committee:

- *Pros*: Discussion, conference calls, and decisions can be better managed, meetings can be less structured, and greater intimacy is possible.
- *Cons*: More work will have to be done by fewer people, there may be less of a cross section of the congregation represented, and some skills may be less available.

Approaching Prospective Search Committee Members

Preferably, the board selects the individuals asked to serve. If your bylaws or church order requires a congregational vote to approve search committee members, follow those requirements. A letter similar to the sample below should be sent by the board secretary to each person being asked to serve. It should explain why he or she is being asked to serve, and it should identify his or her tasks. Modify the letter to meet your specific actions.

> The Anytown Community Church board took action last night to approve the formation of a pastoral search committee to manage the search for a new pastor. Additionally, we approved a list of people to be on this committee. Individuals were approved based on their perceived gifts and their unique perspectives that would help to create a well-rounded committee. If you agree to serve on this committee, you will be entrusted with a great responsibility. We have confidence in you and believe you would be a valuable member of our search committee.
>
> You are asked to reflect on the requirements to serve in this capacity, since the committee must work intimately together. Our expectations of all committee members are:

- to be in constant prayer for Anytown Community Church and the search process
- to be a dedicated attendee of Anytown Community Church and its functions
- to know Anytown Community Church's strengths and weaknesses
- to take the necessary time to be prepared for meetings
- to be dedicated to attending the committee's meetings
- to respect confidences

Our prayer is that you consider this request in two ways. First, commit yourself to prayer to know God's will, and second, if you are married, discuss this request with your spouse, since serving will affect family life.

It is anticipated that meetings will be held biweekly at the start but could become more frequent as information is gathered about available and interested pastors. Between meetings there will be varying amounts of time required as work progresses, surveys are conducted, contacts are made, sermon tapes received, and letters sent. We want you to understand the time commitment up front. Depending on your other church-related responsibilities, you may have to evaluate reducing these to allow for the time necessary to serve in this vital role. The search process could typically take between eight months to one year; however, it could extend beyond one year.

I am available to answer questions you may have about this role. You are asked to respond to me no later than _____ [*give a date one week out*]. Our prayers are with you as you consider your potential role in this important challenge to Anytown Community Church.

Follow up the letter with a personal phone call to the prospective search committee members. Be sure you are familiar with the search process so that you can answer any questions that arise. Stress that there are rewards in serving and that many individuals report an increase in their faith as a result of serving on a search committee. The search process rewards those who serve as they become intimate with the life of their church, their denomination, the pastors they work with, and their fellow search committee members. They will also be rewarded with a deep sense of accomplishment. Assure potential search committee members that they will have the full support of board and the congregation.

If the church has gone through a search within the past 10 years, there may be individuals in the church who served on the previous search committee. Consider arranging a meeting with these former search committee members who may provide valuable insights learned from their search.

Prayer and the Search Committee

The pastoral search committee must bathe the search process in prayer. From the beginning, prayer must be an integral part of the process, not something simply done at the start and close of meetings. You may choose to start meetings with a single prayer and close with conversational prayer. Respect those who may feel uncomfortable praying out loud, yet encourage them to join in when they are more comfortable doing so.

The board and the congregation also need to pray regularly for the search committee and the search process. Include the work of the search committee in congregational prayers and in prayer requests during worship services. When there are specific immediate needs, activate your church's prayer chain if you have one. If you do not have a prayer chain, consider starting one to support the search committee.

The search committee must understand the role of prayer in discerning the Spirit's leading. Pause, reflect in silence, and then pray before decisions are made, when the path is uncertain, when tensions build, and when praise is due. Each committee member must commit to pray daily for their fellow committee members, for the search process, and for the pastors with whom they are interacting. You will often feel the urge to hurry the process, and focusing on prayer will properly ground you in the Spirit. God will honor your prayers for guidance.

Remember that for every pastor who moves, another church becomes vacant. Another search committee will be formed and the whole search process repeated. Your success in finding the pastor to lead you is a loss for his or her former church. That church also needs to be remembered in your prayers. As you grieved when your pastor left, their members too will grieve. Consider writing a letter to their board and search committee after your new pastor arrives, letting them know you are praying for them.

As your search committee considers pastors, you will become very close to some of them. Let the pastors whom you have not selected know that you will continue to pray for them as they continue their ministry in their churches. Some pastors will do a reevaluation of their ministry after not getting a call and decide to stay in their current church. Others will continue their search for a new church. Those pastors with whom you communicated for months, who shared deeply of themselves but who did not receive a call from you, will appreciate your support. They all need your prayers.

Search Committee Basics

It must be stressed that all members of the search committee adhere to strict confidentiality standards. The names of pastors being considered must be kept in confidence. When asking pastors to complete questionnaires or when conducting telephone or face-to-face interviews, state up front that confidentiality will be respected.

Search committee materials, such as minutes with details of pastors, pastoral profiles, and questionnaires, and notes from interviews, must all be kept confidential while the committee functions and then properly disposed of when no longer needed. Confidentiality becomes more difficult as the search widens and the search committee tries to keep the congregation as informed as possible, but it must be maintained for the sake of the search process and the pastors involved.

Search committees should have current copies of their regional or denominational church directories and magazines. These publications are a good source of names and contacts. If your denomination has a manual of church order or policies, a constitution, an official letter of call, or compensation guidelines, order copies. Some denominations have a packet of resources for search committees. Inquire about these resources at your regional or denominational offices. You must be aware of any denominational materials that affect how your search committee may operate.

Developing Pastoral Search Committee Guidelines

It is wise to develop guidelines under which the search committee will operate. These guidelines will provide the basis for all that the search committee does. Investigate whether your denomination has guidelines for a search committee. The board may provide input for the guidelines or may let the search committee develop them. Committee goals, commitment, process and procedures, accountability, and expenses might be covered in the guidelines. Specific processes and procedures might be developed for determining who you are as a church, for determining the evaluation and selection criteria, and for presenting the nominated pastor(s) for a congregational vote. Sample guidelines covering these areas might look like the one below. Make your guidelines conform to your denomination's guidelines for the search process.

1. The search committee pledges to pray daily for its task and for each member of the committee.
2. The search committee will conduct a search process that is to result in a prioritized list of pastors to be considered for a call to Anytown Community Church. The search committee will make recommendations to the board for approval. The names will be submitted to the congregation and a call extended to the one selected.
3. The search committee will submit regular progress reports to the board and the congregation.
4. Routine expenses will require committee approval, and invoices will be submitted to the church treasurer for payment.
5. As part of the search process, the committee may prepare the following materials including:

    - congregational questionnaire
    - the denominational church profile
    - church information packet
    - advertising
    - pastoral search budget
    - pastoral questionnaire
    - procedures for interviews
    - procedures for checking references
    - procedures for personality and relationship testing
    - compensation package
    - pastoral job description or a definition of roles, responsibilities, and relationships
    - search flow chart

Clarify with the board what your authority and accountability will be for your committee's work and expenses. Determine what types of expenses require the board's approval and if there are limits on how much you may spend without preapproval.

Setting Ground Rules

When first meeting as a committee, consider establishing some basic ground rules for the meetings and the process. These may pertain to how the committee functions and how it supports one another. Examples of ground rules to consider include:

- Our search is founded on prayer.
- Members commit to pray daily for committee members and their work.
- We will meet in a member's home. (A home usually provides a warmer atmosphere than a room at the church and helps to build community.)
- Meetings will start at the scheduled time.
- Members are responsible for completing the tasks assigned to them.
- Decisions will be made by consensus.
- Committee members will act with trust, integrity, and honesty.
- Decisions on which pastor to call will not be made until all the information is received on all the pastors being considered at that stage of the process.
- The search committee will not rush the search process.

Meetings, Agendas, and Minutes

Initially, the search committee may choose to meet biweekly. However, when there are pastors in the interview stages and the search is narrowing down, weekly meetings will be necessary. When pastors are finally invited to visit and preach to the congregation (if allowed by your denominational rules), special meetings may have to be planned. The visit will then have to be reviewed, a decision made about the candidate, and plans made for the next visiting pastor. All these different pieces of the search puzzle must fit together in order to move towards a final selection.

Agendas and minutes need to be distributed in a timely manner. It is helpful for committee members to have agendas prior to a scheduled meeting in order to plan and review material attached or previously distributed. The secretary may put together the agenda alone or with the help of the chairperson. An agenda early in the search process will differ from one after months of search and communication. Each new agenda needs to be built from the minutes of the previous meeting, with thought given to new items or issues as the committee moves forward. As committee members become more intensely involved in the search process, allow time in the agenda for their care and support. Plan for a short time of worship together at each meeting.

Minutes of all meetings need to be distributed soon after the meeting in order that committee members may review both what they did and follow up on any actions they are responsible for prior to the next meeting. The minutes need to be both concise and complete. They serve as a summary of what the search committee's actions and decisions were and what was heard, discussed, and decided about each pastor considered. Action items that require follow-through by committee members can be italicized for emphasis, with the appropriate person's name noted. Since it is helpful for the committee to see in the minutes what stage a particular pastor is in, consider providing a sheet that shows all the pastors considered and where they are in the search process. The chapter "Communications with Pastors" gives an example of such a chart. Minutes should be given to the president or chair of the board and any items that require board approval should be noted. Minutes may also be sent to the pastor acting as your supervisor or counselor, and to other individuals or committees with oversight responsibilities. Minutes are to be treated as confidential and should not be distributed to others or posted for the congregation to read.

Each search committee member should have an adequate system and materials to manage the flow of paperwork. Give consideration to purchasing two- or three-inch binders for all members, with tabs for specific topics. Pastors' profiles should be filed alphabetically by their last names. As pastors are discussed and profiles reviewed, all material and notes on any given pastor should be filed with his or her profile. Decisions will be made at various points in the process. If the decision is made to terminate communication with a particular pastor, committee members should remove his or her profile from their binders and store it apart from the active pastors' profiles. Possible tab headings are as follows:

- Minutes and Agendas
- Search Committee Guidelines
- The Call Process and Call Letter
- Congregational Questionnaire
- Church Profile
- Church Information Packet
- Pastoral Questionnaire
- Pastoral Profiles
- Hosting Visiting Pastors

- Selection and Evaluation Criteria
- Congregational Updates
- Church Supervisor/Counselor
- Regional/Denominational Correspondence

Managing Search Expenses

Since most pastoral vacancies are unplanned, churches typically do not have a budget for a newly formed search committee. Several options exist, depending on how structured your budget and finances are. If you will not be paying a full-time interim specialist, an effective method is to take the amount of money normally budgeted for the pastor's salary and expenses and put it into a budget for pastoral search expenses. Expense categories might include travel, telephone, correspondence, and miscellaneous items. Expenses for a part-time interim minister or for guest pastors could be also charged to that budget. Another less efficient option is to simply charge expenses against an existing budget category. However, this method makes it harder to distinguish between search expenses and the regular church expenses in that category.

Your Church Supervisor/Counselor

It is the duty of the church board to notify your regional or denominational offices that your pastor will be leaving as of a certain date. In many cases, the denominational office will take the initiative and assign a supervisor, counselor, or synodical staff member to your church. These individuals are selected and trained based on their leadership gifts and skills. They should make themselves available to the search committee and the board for assistance. You need to work with the supervisor/counselor, asking him or her to attend search committee meetings whenever possible to provide input regarding your process. When a pastor is ultimately called, this person might also sign the letter of call, if required by your denomination. Many supervisors or counselors will have a broad knowledge of pastors in the region or denomination and might, according to your denomination's practices, make suggestions about which pastors to consider and provide input on those about whom you have received information. He or she can give insights on a range of topics from how you present pastors to the congregation to providing an adequate compensation package for the new pastor. If your search committee is well organized, you may function well with little contact and advice from the supervisor or counselor; however, it is his or her responsibility to be certain that you are managing the process well. When the new pastor is selected, the supervisor or counselor might also have a role in moving the selection through any denominational or regional processes for approval and assisting in the installation service.

The newly formed search committee has a huge challenge facing it that will not be easy. In the absence of a pastor, the congregation needs to be managed on many different levels and kept informed about the search process. Once the committee determines how to handle these tasks, it will be free to move on to the more complex areas of the search process.

Task Cluster: The Pastoral Search Committee

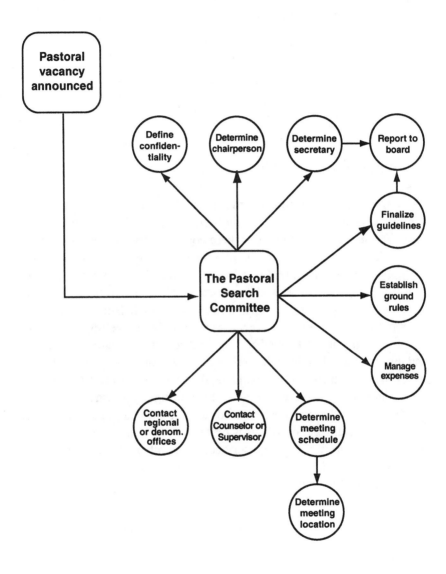

CHAPTER 2

Managing the Congregation

Keeping Information Current

The congregation needs to know the basics about what the pastoral search committee is doing. Not all of the details need to be shared, but the congregation does need to know where you are in the process of finding a pastor. A congregation that is uninformed is typically confused or unsupportive. Tell them that you have reviewed "x" number of profiles, have scheduled interviews, and have moved "x" number of pastors into the next stage of the process. Put an announcement or a half-page insert in the bulletin on the Sunday after each search committee meeting. If there is a church bulletin board located in a central location, create an attractive, readable display that includes relevant data from your congregational survey, the search committee mandate, the search committee member list, and updates on the search process. In addition, the search committee chairperson, or other key person, needs to keep the congregation informed with periodic status reports. This is best done with announcements during the Sunday morning worship service. Remember not to compromise confidentiality standards. The sample bulletin insert below is an example of how information can be shared.

Pastoral Search Committee Report

Updates for December 13

Stage IV: Interviews
Interviews have been arranged with two pastors who have advanced to this stage.

Stage III: Sermon Tapes and Reference Checks
We are talking to the references provided to us by five pastors. Sermon tapes have been requested, and three have been received so far and are being reviewed.

Stage II: Pastoral Profiles and Questionnaires
We have reviewed the pastoral questionnaires of two additional pastors, and at least one of these will be moving to stage III.

Stage I: Sharing and Gathering Information
We are at stage I with two pastors who have been sent packets of information about our church and are completing our questionnaire and sending sermon tapes.

We have discussed 22 additional pastors and have found that they are not open to a move at this time or are not a good match for us.

Our next meeting on January 9 will focus on the visiting schedule for the candidates and on the selection process.

Keeping the congregation informed can be simple, but everyone wants information in various degrees of depth. Some just want to know that the committee is doing its job. Others want to know that the committee has talked to the pastor whom they recommended. A few will want to know everything. All search committee members need to be mindful of confidentiality issues when sharing information about the search process. Remember that the names of pastors under consideration should not be shared with the congregation. Use a weekly bulletin announcement like the one below in order to keep the lines of communication open.

Pastoral Search Questions ? ? ?

Any member of the Search Committee would be happy to provide answers to your questions about the search process, potential pastors, time frames, and the call process. Just ask one of us. [*Include names and telephone numbers of committee members*]

When the search process has reached the point of selecting a possible pastor, more information needs to be given to the congregation. Church members need to know the dates that pastors will be visiting and be encouraged to be present to hear them and meet them. They also need to know how the pastor will be selected and the dates of any planned congregational meetings. Create a handout for the congregation with a page that describes the selection process, lists those candidates who have been selected and their visiting schedule, and gives the date of the congregational meeting. Attach a page about each pastor. Make up an information page on each pastor that contains information on the pastor's gifts, strengths, ministry style, his or her thoughts on worship, leadership, education, evangelism, fellowship, the person's pastoral history, a family profile, and a family picture (if available). More information on this step in the search process can be found in the chapter "Presenting Your Best Side."

Pastoral Support during the Interim

While the pastoral search is underway, the search committee needs to be able to focus all its energies on the search. The board's priority needs to be the maintaining of responsible church leadership during the period in which the church is vacant. How best to lead the congregation in their spiritual walk and their ministries needs to be thought through. Ministry must continue. The decision to use an interim pastor or guest pastors during the vacancy will usually be made by the church board, but the search committee can provide input. Some denominations require churches to have an interim pastor for a specific time period before starting the search process. This allows time for healing and for reflection on who they are and what they need.

While the congregation is without a pastor, it has several options for pastoral support. Understanding these options will help the board and the search committee decide what their preference is for ministry support.

- First, your denominational or regional offices can be contacted to determine if there is a trained interim pastor available to serve your church.
- Second, pastors who are not specifically trained in interim ministry can also be contacted to serve for a specific time period.
- Third, the board can decide to use local pastors, or perhaps retired pastors, as weekly guest pastors.

Trained interim pastors, sometimes called transition specialists, will provide the best support. They have been trained to help a congregation end its relationship with the previous pastor, conduct self-study and discern new directions, identify and develop new lay leaders, rethink denominational relationships, and build commitment to a new future. Trained interim pastors can be especially helpful in situations in which the previous pastor left after an unusually long tenure or in a storm of controversy surrounding some form of pastor malfeasance. Both trained interim pastors and other pastors who can serve until a permanent pastor is chosen can provide the congregation with a sense of continuity that is not felt by using weekly guest pastors, and both can provide a good base of support to the search committee as it works through pastoral questions. They are often eager to visit with members and friends. Interim pastors also are able to attend your board and elder meetings to provide advice and support. A retired pastor, although not necessarily trained in interim ministry, is often able to stay and work in the church for a specific length of time. These pastors usually provide only maintenance ministry–preaching and teaching and doing pastoral care. Whether you use one or several interim pastors, you will want to develop a contract that specifies their level of involvement with the board, committees, and member visitation.

If weekly guest pastors are your choice, your board, usually through the elders, is responsible for filling the pulpit on Sundays at your church's expense. Guest pastors might include a pastor from a church with multiple pastors, a pastor assigned by a regional office to provide service for one Sunday, or a retired pastor. An elder or worship leader will need to coordinate the elements of the worship services as necessary. Cost wise, guest pastors are the cheapest because they typically only provide support for Sunday services. Four Sundays a month could cost between $400 and $800. This includes payment for leading the worship service and mileage expense.

Plan to pay a full-time interim pastor what you paid your previous pastor, including benefits and allowances. If you choose to call a part-time interim pastor, you would be financially responsible for your percentage of his or her time. If you choose to approach a retired pastor to serve your congregation as a long-term pastor, expect to pay a base salary, travel expenses to and from your church, housing, and expenses for local mileage and hospitality. Either regional or denominational offices may have guidelines for payment to pastors based on the various levels of leadership they can provide.

The biggest consideration is the value provided by an interim pastor. An interim pastor can perform whatever tasks he or she mutually agrees upon with the board. If there is healing to be done, if the leadership could use the insights of a pastor, if visiting is helpful, or if continuity in the pulpit is important, try to obtain an interim pastor.

Your judicatory or denominational liaison will be able to provide names of trained, interim ministers or other pastors available for long-term service. A retired pastor might be willing to commit to three to six months of service, and an interim pastor up to eighteen months or more of service. In either case, if necessary, line up another pastor to follow the first. The benefits of having an interim pastor far outweigh the additional costs. You and your congregation will be blessed many times over. The service of an experienced, retired pastor can also be extremely helpful.

The Grieving Process

When a pastor leaves a church, members and friends will have varying emotions to deal with. People may feel denial that their pastor would consider leaving, anger when they realize that he or she is leaving, guilt because they feel some burden of personal responsibility for his or her departure, fear for what will happen to their church, or relief if they did not like him or her. Some people may even go through stages of depression. Others may pull away from the church and ultimately even leave. This grieving process is normal.

The search committee needs to work with the board to be sure the congregation's grieving process is managed well. While this is more the concern of the board than the search committee, if it is not managed properly, it can hinder the work of the search committee. Assistance may be needed from your church supervisor or counselor, from neighboring pastors, or if necessary, from a counseling service. Members need to deal with their emotional ties to the former pastor. If there are any unresolved issues from the previous pastor that involve members or friends of the congregation, they need to be resolved.

The elders in particular need to be sensitive to the need of members to grieve. They should encourage open communication between the board and the congregation and among members. Visits or telephone calls should be made to members whom they suspect need their attention. Help members talk through their feelings and work through unresolved issues. Arrange for counseling when necessary. Realize that this grieving process needs to take place in order to allow individuals to attain closure with their feelings for their previous pastor.

Unresolved grief, issues, or problems can easily work against the search committee. They can adversely influence the results of congregational surveys and affect your list of desired qualities of a new pastor. Search committee members, in particular, need to be aware of their personal grieving and deal with it early in the search process.

When it knows how to manage the congregation effectively, the search committee can begin its study of the board, congregation, and the ministries of the church. This process is important to assure a good match with your next pastor.

Task Cluster: Managing the Congregation

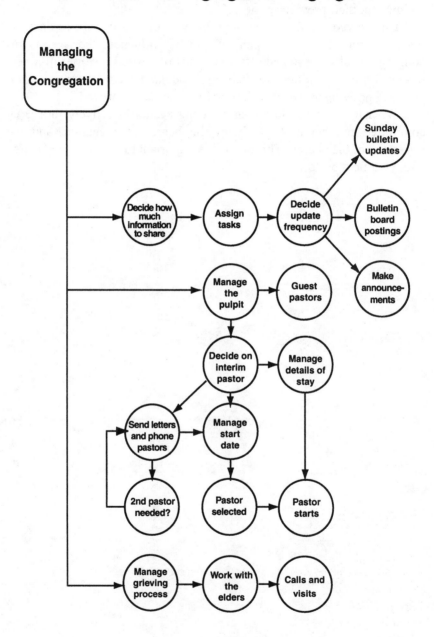

CHAPTER 3

Determining Who You Are

Pastors' Perspectives

The information you present about your church–its leadership, membership, and ministries–must be as thorough and accurate as you can compile. Surveyed pastors gave the following perspectives about the way churches described themselves. Consider their comments as you think about determining who you are as a church.

- "I preferred churches with vision, purpose, and goals, and that knew who they were and where they hoped to go."
- "They knew who they were and presented that information in a customized church profile and church packet."
- "They did not always identify all of the informal leadership."
- "They did not identify their weaknesses. They did not mislead in their impressions; they simply did not have the answers to give."

The Importance of Determining Who You Are

One of the most important tasks that your pastoral search committee will undertake is a self-study of the board, congregation, and ministries of the church. It is certainly not the task of only the search committee to work through all of these issues; the board also needs to be directly involved in this process. The study is necessary in order to portray your church accurately to a prospective pastor through your information packet and in other communications. Use this study to identify the church's strengths and weaknesses as well as many other characteristics. This should be done through an information gathering process managed by the search committee. The information provided to pastors will give them a definitive statement of your focus, needs, and priorities. Do not paint a false picture of who you are. Anything incorrect will surface when the pastor gives serious consideration to the call, or after he or she accepts the call and discovers that things are not as rosy as initially portrayed. In any case, the pastor and the board will have to work through the issues.

Remember that pastors will read your church packet in the same way that you read their pastoral profiles. Just as you read between the lines, so will they. Just as you are alert for red flags, so are they. Just as you check references, so may they. Let your creative juices flow as you build your church packet and make a church video, but be both complete and realistic. Consider the following questions in determining who you are as a church.

- What is unique about our congregation?
- What is unique about our opportunities for ministry?
- What are the strengths and weaknesses of our congregation?
- Are we open to change? How do we convey our openness or lack of openness?
- What challenges can we offer to a pastor?
- What in our past is especially useful as we look ahead at new challenges?
- What is our vision and our mission, and does our congregation own them?
- What core values form our ministries?
- What is our view on outreach, and do our actions support this view?
- What ministries need to be started or developed more fully?
- What would we anticipate as our needs over the next five years?
- Is our church willing to learn from and follow the leadership of a new pastor?
- What professional qualities and attributes are we looking for in a pastor?

Talk to your board about the vision, mission, and core value statements you have in place. Are they current? Can the majority of the congregation identify them? Do they need to be reworked? While the search committee focuses on the self-study, the board should focus on these statements.

An area that is becoming more important in the search process is the identification of issues that could, if unidentified in the search process, affect the relationship between the church and a new pastor. These issues may be about styles of worship, about leadership, or about women in office. Failure to identify them could lead to problems in the relationship between the pastor and board or the pastor and congregation. A pastor who is used to leading independently could end up with problems in a church where the board has shared church leadership with its former pastor. Similarly, a pastor who enjoys seeker-sensitive worship services will feel stifled in a congregation that is used to liturgical worship. Be aware of issues in your church and describe them in your church profile and the church information packet distributed to prospective pastors. You will also want to ask questions about these issues on your pastoral questionnaire.

Your congregation might use the self-study process to clarify other aspects of your ministry. For example, some churches have several pastors. There may be a senior pastor, a youth pastor, a pastor of evangelism, or a pastor of congregational care. Other churches may call a pastor for a mission field ministry. Another church may call a pastor to be a college or military chaplain or to be a pastor in an industrial ministry. If you are calling a pastor to a specialized ministry, think through the needs you hope the new pastor will help you address and your specific expectations about that pastor's role. By identifying your unique pastoral needs, you will make it easier for pastors to decide whether your ministry needs could fit their experience, gifts, and skills.

Through a self-study and identification of issues, you will have taken the first steps towards ensuring a potentially good match with a new pastor. The second step will be to clarify expectations that you may have of your new pastor and that he or she may have of the board and congregation. Will the pastor be expected to do counseling, serve on five committees, and teach Sunday school and midweek Bible studies? Does the pastor expect board members to lead the committees? Each may have expectations of the other in areas of commitment, involvement, and accountability. The sample "Pastoral Responsibilities, and Relationships" in appendix G is one tool you can use to clarify pastoral expectations. Similar tools can be made for board members and the congregation. Care taken in these two steps can help avoid later problems with relationships in the ministry life of the pastor, the board, and the congregation.

Congregational Surveys

A congregational survey, the most commonly used self-study method, will provide information about your church that you need to know in order to determine if a pastor might be a good fit for your church. In appendix A is a sample congregational survey, which can be modified to fit your congregation's requirements. The survey covers five specific areas.

- Personal information about the person completing the survey
- Desired professional qualities you want your next pastor to excel in
- Expectations you have of your next pastor
- Strengths, weaknesses, and needs of your congregation
- Congregational interests—what is important to you

There are many reasons to do a congregational survey. You will want to conduct one if you meet any of the following criteria.

- You do not know the demographics of your congregation.
- You are uncertain of the professional qualities you desire in your next pastor.
- You are unsure of the congregation's expectations regarding what a new pastor should be involved in.
- You cannot identify the needs in your congregation.
- You cannot identify your strengths and weaknesses.

If your church has recently completed a similar type of survey or gone through a master planning or strategic planning effort, this survey may not be necessary. If you conduct a congregational survey anyway, compare the results with your master planning or strategic planning summaries to determine if all areas are covered and if the results match. If the results do not match, take the time to find the correct information by talking to key people, taking another survey, or inviting the congregation to an open forum. Once a survey has been completed and tabulated, be sure to post the results for the congregation to see.

The Church Profile Form

If your congregation belongs to a denomination, you may find that the denomination has a church profile form. Request a copy and review it to be sure your survey asks for all the information needed to complete the church profile form. When you have completed your self-study and survey, you should be able to complete the profile describing your church and the type of pastor for whom you are searching. Use this church profile form to prepare your church information packet. You will also submit copies of the completed form to the required denominational or regional offices. It is this form that they will use to provide you with pastors' names for consideration. Finally, your board should be given a copy for its records.

If you do not belong to a denomination that has a church profile form, use the questions below as a guide to compile the information typically requested on a profile form. Again, the information will be helpful as you develop your church information packet.

The typical church profile form asks for basic information about your church:

- What is the size of the staff? What are staff titles, and are the positions full- or part-time?
- What is the size of the board, its gender breakdown, and its makeup (elders, deacons, or committee leaders)?
- What are your vision, mission, and core values?
- What are your current and future congregational goals?
- What is the church membership (include yearly numbers for the past ten years)?
- What is your style of worship and how many are in attendance?
- What is your church education program and what curriculum do you use?
- What programs are offered for children, youth, singles, and adults?

Other questions may address your facilities and budget:

- What is the present budget and amount of indebtedness?
- Do you usually meet your yearly budget?
- What is the condition of the church facilities?
- Does the church own a parsonage?
- Is it an option for the pastor to own his or her own home?

Be able to identify the specifics about the congregation and the community:

- What are the congregation's strengths and weaknesses?
- What are the congregation's interests?
- What are the needs of the community?
- What is your involvement in the community?
- What are your outreach ministries?
- What ecumenical ministries is the church involved in?

And finally, be able to answer questions about your next pastor:

- What are the personal and professional qualities you desire in your next pastor?
- What are your expectations of the next pastor?
- What is your compensation package?

As the search committee goes through the self-study process and conducts a congregational survey, it is forming an excellent base of knowledge about its church and ministries. The next step in the search process is to use this information to create your church information packet.

Task Cluster: Determining Who You Are

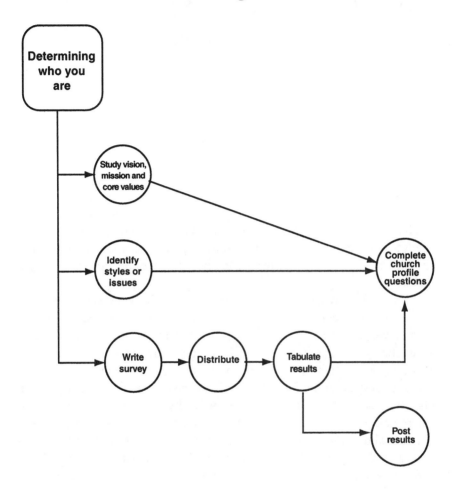

CHAPTER 4

The Church Information Packet

The Value of Quality

A church information packet contains everything an interested pastor needs to know about your church. It must help him or her identify with your church and want to explore further the possibility of becoming your next pastor.

Think about what kind of church information packet you would like to create. It would certainly be easy to produce a mediocre packet with a night's work. However, will it present an accurate picture of the degree of excellence your church pursues? Is it going to grab the interest of a pastor so that he or she wants to learn more about your church? You need to create a high-quality church information package, customized for your church. It may take several weeks and many hours by different people in your congregation, but because of the various perspectives, it will speak volumes about who you are. Above all else, be honest in how you represent your church and ministries, and describe its strengths and needs. Think about how you can express what is unique to your church–something that sets your church apart from other churches. Build on this unique element.

Quality can also be demonstrated in other ways. Send your packets by priority mail. This will cost about one-third as much as express mail and yet arrive in only two to three days. Include a self-addressed, stamped envelope for the return of the package in case the pastor has no interest in your query. If there are forms or questionnaires for the pastor to return if he or she is interested, be sure to include a self-addressed, stamped envelope for that purpose. Be clear, direct, and concise as you write the material for your packet. Make a well-organized packet. By presenting a quality packet, you will demonstrate that you care about your congregation and your ministries. Remember that a quality package will invite a quality response.

What to Include

The most logical starting question is, "How much do we need to include in our church information packet?" Another way to approach this task is to think about what you want to say about your church. What would be important for a stranger to know about you? How much does it take? Realize that other churches are also creating church information packets to send to pastors. Remember that too little information in a packet is worse than too much.

Information that describes your board, congregation, ministries, and community should be included in the church packet. The areas listed below are key to providing a complete picture of who you are as a church. Ideally, put each of the areas below on a separate page, writing enough about each to satisfy a pastor who knows nothing about your church. Consider using a folder with a three-hole paper clasp in the center and pockets on either side. Typed sheets can be placed in the center section, and smaller brochures or booklets will fit in the pockets. This type of folder best displays the material you will send.

Much of this information can be gathered through congregational surveys, master planning or strategic planning documents, church brochures, board minutes, and area profiles from newspapers and local business associations. Church bulletins, newsletters, special event programs, and telephone directories will complete your information files.

Our Vision, Mission, and Goals. If your church has a vision and/or mission statement(s), include them in the packet. Some churches have a statement of core values. Other statements that guide ministries or committees can also be included. These all serve to show the focus of the congregation. What is the energy level in the church toward the vision and mission? If a visiting pastor were to randomly question a few members, would they be able to identify the vision and/or mission of the church? Do you have goals for the church and the committees? Review and update any that are outdated or have been found to be unrealistic.

Our Worship Style. Identify your worship style. Is it traditional, contemporary, or a mix? Do you use hymns or praise songs? Is the main source of music an organ, piano, or keyboard? Are there choirs or praise teams? Do you have a band or use musical instruments in worship? Who plans worship? Does someone other than the pastor lead portions of the service?

Our Congregation. This section can feature information about the diversity of the congregation, including the number in worship, church growth information, how long various percentages of members and visitors have been affiliated with your church, age make-up of the congregation, percentages of members living different distances from the church, the ethnic percentages represented, and the mix of occupations represented. If your denomination provides a standard profile form, use it; otherwise choose a format that matches the rest of the information packet.

Our Structure. In this section define your church's organization. Identify the structure of the board and the number of elders and deacons. Explain your committee structure. If you have any policy manuals, structure manuals, or other organizational guidelines, briefly discuss them. Identify your staff, the hours they work, and to whom they are accountable. If the role of women in the church is an issue, identify your congregation's position and the role of women serving as leaders on the board and in the congregation. If there are other issues in the church, identify them so they do not come as a surprise to an incoming pastor.

Our Organizational Chart. If you have an organizational chart, include it here. It may be a formal, computer-generated flow chart, or a simple, hand-drawn picture. Either way, it is helpful for a pastor to see the reporting and organizational structure of the board and the committees, and their ministry responsibilities.

Our Strengths and Weaknesses. This section needs to identify known strengths and weaknesses of the congregation based on your congregational survey and self-analysis. You should be able to list at least six strengths and four weaknesses. Be honest. Focus more on the strengths than on the weaknesses. Any unique challenges facing the congregation can also be noted here.

Our Pastoral Ministry Needs. Identify your pastoral ministry needs in the areas of worship, leadership, congregational care, fellowship, and outreach. Identify other areas that may be relevant to your congregation. Consider making a statement section using this format: "Because . . . , we need . . ." If you have completed a standard denominational profile form, this section may duplicate some of that information, but it can be helpful to pastors to hear about your pastoral needs in your own words.

Pastoral Responsibilities and Relationships. If you have a pastoral job description or guidelines, include them here. Appendix G, "Pastoral Responsibilities and Relationships," identifies areas of leadership, authority, commitment, vision development, personal giftedness, equipping and enabling, and relationships to board, staff, and committee leaders. This important section helps a pastor understand his or her areas of responsibility, especially as compared to the leadership responsibilities of the board, staff, and committee leaders listed in the sections below. If you have such a document, incorporate it here. Are you looking for a pastor to be your leader, enabler, or counselor? Do you want a pastor who can teach certain Christian education classes? Identify areas of specialized pastoral ministry he or she may be involved in or responsible for.

Board Responsibilities and Relationships. If you have any guidelines or standards for board members, identify them. It can be helpful for a pastor to know to what standards the board members are held accountable. If you have a pastoral relations committee, describe what function that group serves.

Staff Responsibilities and Relationships. Staff positions should have well-defined job descriptions. For all staff members, include what they are responsible for, to whom they are accountable, and by whom they are supervised. It is helpful for a pastor to know ahead of time what staff oversight roles he or she may have.

Committee Leader Responsibilities and Relationships. Under what standards do committee leaders operate? To whom are they are responsible and accountable? Are their roles clearly defined?

Congregation's Responsibilities and Relationships. To what standards are members held? Are there areas of ministry, commitment, accountability, and relationships to which they are challenged?

Friends of the Congregation. If you have any statements or guidelines for nonmember friends of the congregation, identify them. Identify the number and make-up of the individuals and families who are regular attendees but who have not formally joined the church.

Our Ministries. List all the ministries of your church with a brief sentence or two about each. Consider boys' and girls' clubs, vacation Bible school, church school or Sunday school, the church's preschool, women's and men's groups, junior high and high school youth groups, children's worship, Bible studies, fellowship groups, outreach programs, and youth and adult choirs.

Our Facilities. Describe your facilities. How large is the sanctuary? How many classrooms are there? What is the size of the fellowship hall? How modern are the facilities? Is there off-street parking? Does the church own any other property? Are there any building or expansion plans in the works? Have the facilities been adequately maintained? Consider including photos of the church facilities.

Our Finances. What is the annual budget? Is it usually met? By what percent did giving exceed expenses or fall short of expenses for last year and this current year. Describe trends of giving patterns over the past five years. Identify the major pieces of the budget picture. Are there any outstanding debt obligations and if so, what are the anticipated time frames to pay off the debt?

Our Pastoral Compensation Policy. Some churches follow compensation standards set by their denominations. Others build their own compensation packages. What source has been used to establish guidelines for pastoral salary and benefits? What is included in benefits? What expenses are reimbursed? Is there continuing education money and time built into the package? Is there a parsonage? If so, include photos and details. Is the church agreeable to the idea of the pastor owning his or her own home? If a finance committee manages the compensation package, be sure your information is current. Determine if you want to provide fixed numbers or a range of numbers at this time, or if you want to wait until a call is issued to assign amounts to each part of the proposed compensation package.

Our History. Write a page or two about the history of your church. In story format, tell what has happened. Identify previous pastors and years of service. Have there been areas of specific focus? What events have shaped the congregation, the mission, or the vision? Have there been building projects? If you have a church historian, ask him or her to write a good history of the congregation. Some churches have church anniversary booklets that contain a history of the congregation.

Our Community. Describe your community. What type of neighborhood is the church located in? What similar churches are nearby? What is the general area like? What variety of Christian and public schools are available? Are there any colleges and/or universities nearby? What opportunities exist for culture, sports, and outdoor activities?

Search Committee, Board, and Staff Contacts. List the members of the search committee, the board, and staff by name and title. A few sentences about each person's role in the congregation will help to personalize who they are. Include committee members' phone numbers only if you are open to prospective pastors contacting any or all individuals directly; otherwise, give the phone numbers only for those individuals designated as contacts.

Additional Materials. The materials below can be added to the pockets on the sides of the folder. Select materials appropriate for your church.

- Two or three recent programs or bulletins
- Two or three recent church newsletters
- A church directory, if you have one with photos
- Brochures about the church's ministries
- Brochures from the church's special Christmas, Easter, or musical programs
- Brochures from local Christian schools
- A note asking for a photo
- A pastoral questionnaire (if allowed by your denomination) that the pastor can complete if interested in continuing communications, and a return envelope
- An addressed and stamped envelope for the return of the packet if the pastor feels your church is not a good fit for his or her gifts and pastoral skills

If at all possible, have a member of your congregation make a videotape to include in your information packet. A well-made videotape will show more to your candidates about your church and congregational life than any other medium. Activities and subjects to videotape include: choir practices, children and youth programs, fellowship groups, vacation Bible school, church school or Sunday school, special choir cantatas; casual interviews with church members; and the church grounds, facilities, and parsonage. Include an introduction of board members and a time for search committee members to be introduced and share their thoughts. Be sure the search committee views the videotape so they know what the candidates will see. Keep it less than an hour in length.

Make at least 10 of these packages. Have them ready to go, prestamped, so all you have to add is the address. You can easily have 10 or more packages out at one time. If more packages are necessary, make additional copies. Remember to keep originals of all the materials. Consider making several copies of your final packet available to the congregation for its review.

Introducing the Packet

Inside the packet, as the first page, add a cover letter to introduce the packet, explain the contents, and explain what will happen next. Use church letterhead. A sample letter follows.

Greetings from Anytown Community Church!

Thank you for being willing to review material about Anytown Community Church. Our pastoral search committee has made a concise package of materials that we hope will provide a clear picture of our church.

Following this letter is an Anytown Community Church information profile that details our church: vision and mission statements, congregation makeup, structure, strengths and weaknesses, pastoral ministry needs, related responsibilities and relationships, ministries, goals, organizational chart, facilities, finances, pastoral compensation policy, history, community, and a list of contact names and numbers. We trust it will provide answers to your questions.

In the side pockets of this folder are copies of Anytown Community Church brochures, recent Sunday bulletins, two recent monthly newsletters, and information on local Christian schools. A forty-minute videotape is included that will provide a glimpse of our congregation in action.

If you feel positive about our ministries and would like to pursue further discussions, please complete the pastoral questionnaire found in one of the side pockets and send it to us in the envelope provided. A photo would also be appreciated.

If, however, after reviewing this package, you do not feel comfortable pursuing additional discussions with us, please use the enclosed self-addressed, stamped envelope to return the materials to us. We appreciate your time in considering Anytown Community Church.

A member of the pastoral search committee will be contacting you within 10 days. We pray that through this search process, both you and our congregation will find a match that will honor God and further his kingdom here on earth.

Modify the letter as appropriate, based on constraints or special procedures of your denomination.

With your church information packet completed, you have a powerful resource to send to pastors. If it is complete and thorough, pastors will learn much about your church, people, ministries, and facilities. The next step is to identify pastors who might be candidates. Rarely do pastors come to you. You need to find them.

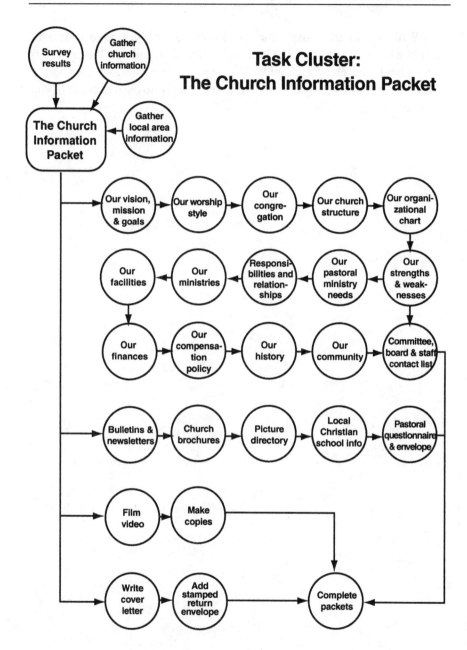

Task Cluster:
The Church Information Packet

CHAPTER 5

Finding Candidates

Sources for Candidates

If your denomination permits its congregations to solicit names of prospective pastors independently, there are numerous sources for candidates that your search committee might consider. You can make search announcements in the church bulletin, in regional and denominational publications, and in religious magazines or newsletters with a wider audience. You can also contact pastors whom you know and ask them about potential names.

Run an announcement in your bulletin asking members to give names of pastors they have heard while on vacation, while visiting family and friends, or that they have heard about from others. Ask the member making the referral why they think this particular pastor might be good for Anytown Community Church. Contact former pastors, former members, and your supervisor or counselor for referrals. Pastors may also contact you directly in response to your announcements or ads, or on a referral from another source.

If you obtain names from regional or denominational offices, be prepared to supply them with your completed church profile form so that they can make good recommendations. Once they have your church profile form, allow several weeks for the first round of names to be sent to you. Thereafter, depending on your polity, you might be able to call the offices directly with requests for new names. Remember that the offices often work with many churches at the same time, so plan accordingly and be patient.

When names are received from sources other than from your regional or denominational offices, contact the appropriate office to determine if the pastor has a profile on file and to request a copy. If a profile is not on file, you might make contact by writing the pastor directly with an interest or inquiry letter or by working through denominational channels. (For sample letters see the section "Sharing and Gathering Information" in the chapter "Communications with Pastors.") If you receive the profile and it is out-of-date, write the pastor and ask for an updated profile if he or she has interest in further communication. It is difficult to get an accurate feeling about pastors, or make a decision about them, if their profiles are more than two years old.

As you move through the search process, many pastors will be recommended to you or will contact you directly. It is helpful at this point to understand which pastors should not be contacted. If a pastor has been in a church for only two or three years, do not put him or her on your list. You would not want a search committee to issue a call to your pastor after such a short time and so need to respect this rule for all concerned. If you are affiliated with a denomination, you may find other policies or church order rules that address when pastors may be approached for a new call.

Remember that not every pastor is interested in your church. Many pastors are happy in the ministry they have and will not entertain a call or even desire to receive information about your church. Respect their wishes.

The Pastoral Profile Form

A pastoral profile form is part of a system that serves to match pastors to churches. The profile form, usually managed by a denominational office, allows pastors to be introduced to vacant or soon to be vacant churches. Be forewarned that not all the pastors with forms on file are actually looking for a change in ministry.

The pastoral profile form is usually a several page document with questions about a pastor's ministry and professional preferences, leadership and management style, and personal information. The form's function is to provide search committees with enough information about the pastor to determine if a match between the pastor and the church may be possible. The form should be viewed as a screening aid to assist search committees in the first stage of their selection process. Review the forms, discussing them as a committee to determine which pastors you want to know more about.

Each form typically begins with questions about personal information: address, family information, total number of years in the ministry, and present ministry location and the number of years there.

Questions may focus on the pastor's ministry preferences including the type of ministry setting (rural, suburban, or metropolitan), geographical area(s) desired, specific type of pastoral ministry, and congregation size.

Other questions will focus on professional preferences in subjects such as preaching and teaching, pastoral calling, youth and elder ministry, counseling, evangelism, community involvement, and congregational focus. Special skills, languages, and continuing education programs may also be listed.

There may also be questions that detail the pastor's personal leadership and management style through the identification of specific qualities and attributes. Examples of qualities and attributes include caring, effectiveness with administration, being good with people, being approachable, taking the initiative, and being sensitive to needs. (For a list of related attributes, see the chapter "Selection Criteria, Evaluation, and Recommendations.")

Pastors may also be asked to identify the schools they attended and degrees earned, personal and professional life stories, published material, influences on their lives, previous careers, and references.

Creating Your Ad

Once you have completed your self-study and congregational survey and written your church profile, you will find a number of uses for the information you gathered. One fruitful process is to try to summarize your findings by describing your congregation in only a few sentences. This exercise is also the first step in creating an advertisement for your church. You are only one church out of many searching for a pastor. There are many other churches at any one time in some stage of the search process. Some denominations allow churches to advertise for a pastor, other do not. If your denomination allows advertising and your church chooses to advertise, denominational, regional, or general religious magazines provide an excellent resource in which to advertise your vacancy. Remember, however, that other churches are doing the same thing. Look through magazines for current ads. Read and critique the following ads.

Somewhere Church in Somewhere, Washington, is seeking a new pastor. Please send inquiries to Search Committee, 123 Here Street, Somewhere, WA 55441

Due to the pending retirement of our pastor of 15 years, Hometown Church is looking for a pastor. Our church profile is available upon request. Contact the Search Committee, Hometown Church, 75 Center Road, Hometown, WA 63225.

Midtown Church invites applications for the position of pastor to succeed the Rev. G. Sermon who is retiring. The Search Committee seeks a pastor with outstanding pulpit strength to effectively present the gospel message. This person should have outstanding pastoral strength to relate to the needs of individual members. Strong administrative skills will help in leading a staff ministry and planning and coordinating worship. Strong visionary leadership will help our church fulfill its mission role in the broader community. Midtown Church has provided an effective, faithful ministry in a suburban setting for over 50 years. Resumes or inquiries should be sent to the Search Committee, 8910 Spirit Street, Midtown, MI 07654.

Anytown Community Church, with 200 members and regular attendees, is now actively seeking a full-time pastor. Located in the East Side, Anytown and its surrounding communities are rich in cultural and ethnic diversity, which is reflected in the congregation and provides considerable potential for outreach and growth. The pastor should enjoy working in a decentralized church structure that is supported by a hard working board, a Christ-centered staff, and active committees. Our worship services are celebratory with strong music and praise emphasis. If you feel God is leading you to this challenge, please send inquiry or profile to: Mark Jordan, 12345 Alive Place, Anytown, CA 00001; ph. 510-555-1010.

Community Church in Walnut, Illinois, is seeking a pastor. We're a suburban congregation of 75 families involved with Christian education and community activities. We seek a pastor committed to preaching and teaching who shares our vision for community service and outreach. Demonstrated leadership as a team builder and skills in reaching youth are also desirable. Please send inquiries or resumes to Search Committee, c/o Tim Lockley, 3232 Alpha Drive, Walnut, IL 60605; ph. 312-555-1111, fax 312-555-1112.

Your task is to create an ad that is honest, warm, and inviting to a pastor who might be actively searching for a church change, or one on the edge of decision making. Did the first two ads catch your eye and make you want to write for more information? Most likely they did not. The third uses a good blend of wording to identify what type of pastor they are looking for, but tells little about the congregation. The fourth ad identifies something about the area, possible opportunities, and a lot about the church and its leadership and worship style. The fifth ad identifies something about the area and congregation, the congregation's focus, and specifics on what they are looking for in a pastor. The last two ads will generate more responses than the first three ads. The last two ads also have a personal name to respond to instead of a impersonal title. A phone number offers a quick way for an interested pastor to make timely contact. If you have them, give your personal E-mail address and fax number for convenience. Many churches are building Web sites on the Internet. If you have a Web site, identify it in your ad.

Using the results of your congregational survey and the information from your church profile form, have several committee members write an ad. Then use the best one or parts of several ads. Be creative, but do not paint a word picture that is inaccurate. As a committee, talk the ad through word by word, thinking about each word and how it fits. This is not a time to save a few dollars with a short ad that says little.

Review denominational, regional, or general religious publications to determine where you want to advertise. Call the advertising department and request a rate sheet and information about special rates for repeat ads. In a monthly magazine run the ad for several months and wait for responses. If you want additional responses, rerun the ad. At any point in your search process, you can choose to rerun or modify the ad. In monthly magazines, because of the lead time necessary for publication, the same ad will typically run for several months. Running the same ad every week for several months in weekly magazines is costly and you might get more and better responses with intermittently run ads. Neither the readership nor the interest of pastors changes that much from week to week.

Do not forget to update your ad as necessary. If you indicate in your ad that you will have a church profile ready by a certain date, update your ad on that date. If a July ad stated, "A church profile will be available in early August," then running the same ad three months later, in November, is a mistake. Failing to update your ad can indicate to readers that you have not received any responses to your initial ad, you are out of touch with what your ad says, or you do not care enough about updating your ad to reflect where you are in your search process.

It is exciting to serve on a pastoral search committee and see how many wonderful men and women God has prepared to lead the church. As you hear about them through your sources and read their profiles, you will be blessed. The next step is to make contact with the pastors.

Task Cluster: Finding candidates

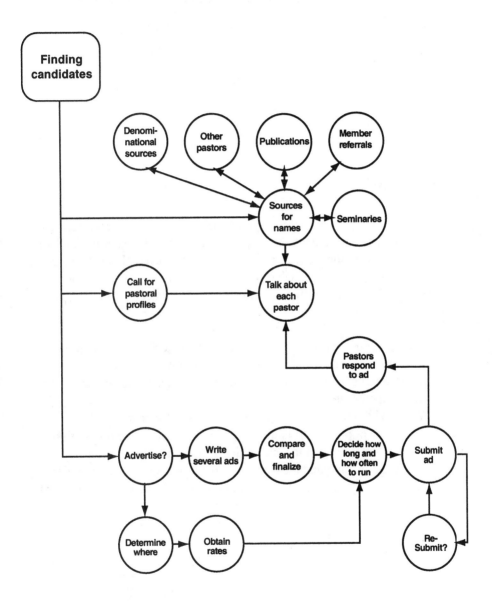

CHAPTER 6

Communications with Pastors

Pastors' Perspectives

Communication can make or break your search effort. First impressions are important, but throughout the search process pastors will be taking stock of how well you communicate. Pastors who were surveyed about the search process were clear about what they considered to be good or bad communication. Consider their comments as you think about how you can communicate better.

- "They provided well-organized and ample materials, making regular, courteous, and caring calls to check on my progress."
- "They kept us informed of how the process was going, including my place in the process."
- "We need to cultivate more trust and respect for pastors."
- "Timing is important—it is difficult to be in a waiting mode with one church when you need to make a decision on another church."
- "There is one thing that is usually in short supply on both sides and that is honesty. Search committees should be willing to ask the hard questions."
- "They should have asked more questions of me in terms of my gifts, strengths, and weaknesses."
- "They should have given me their church profile first, then asked me if I felt at all led to consider their ministry, rather than ask on the phone, throw my name into the hopper, and then send a profile."
- "A monthly letter should inform applicants of the search status. Few things are as frustrating as sending off an application and not hearing back for three months."

Communications

Communications is an area you need to stay on top of at all times. It takes effort to present enough information so that candidates have a clear, concise picture of who you are as a church, where you have been, where you are going, what your strengths and your weaknesses are, how your leadership functions, and what ministries you support. Present a clear and honest picture in your ad, correspondence, church information packet and videotape, during the interview, and when hosting visiting pastors. Decide at the onset what tone your communications will take. Do you want to come across as formal and all business, warm and caring, or a blend of the two?

It is important to remember that in your pastoral search process, you may have contact with any number of pastors, from 2 to 100, depending on your process and the constraints of your denomination. And in that process you will be rejecting all but one! The manner in which you communicate with them, the quality of your search, and the respect you show them are key factors of which every search committee needs to be aware. Your search must provide quality care equally to the pastors you favor as well as those you pass over. Every pastor should come away from your search process with good things to say about your church. Taking a few minutes from time to time in your meetings to see things from their perspectives and through their eyes and ears can be a good exercise.

The Golden Rule should be followed to the letter. Treat pastors as you would want to be treated and you will be on your way to a positive relationship. Even if your church does not call the pastor, he or she will remember the fair treatment they received. Pastors desire respect and courtesy, just like you and I. Consider the following ways to show them respect and courtesy. These topics will be addressed as we move through the search process.

- Treat them fairly and care for them as they go through the process.
- In your correspondence and when talking to them, respect them for who they are, their leadership potential, their ministry gifts, and their vision.
- Listen to them as they share their personal journeys, their views on the questions you ask, their perspectives on how their ministry skills would fit in your church, and on how important their families are in making a church move.

- Tell them why you want them.
- Give them an honest presentation about your church and its ministry, including problem areas.
- Do not judge them without giving them opportunity to respond.
- Realize that they have churches which require their time, and they cannot drop everything to complete a lengthy questionnaire or to attend a meeting on a moment's notice.
- Pick up their expenses and manage the details when they come for a visit.
- Include their spouses in the interviews and conference calls, at least for part of the time, and allow them both to meet with the elders when you talk about the life of your church.
- Focus on honesty, trust, and open communication.

You need to be proactive, taking the initiative in making phone calls, supplying information before it is requested, and anticipating questions before they are asked. You need to work hard to save pastors the expense and trouble of trying to reach someone on the committee. Decide how you will keep the pastors informed about your search process. Plan on sending out periodic updates or making telephone calls to pastors in the advanced stages of the process, advising them where you are in the search process and how they fit into the overall picture. Let them know why you are still interested in them.

During the search process, an easily overlooked factor in communications is the pastor's spouse and children. Pastors have spouses with their own careers, family issues, and children with their unique needs and school and sports commitments—the same as the rest of us. You must consider the needs and interests of the spouse in the materials you prepare, the manner in which you present your church, and in your written and telephone communications. Include him or her in any interviews. Seek out information on his or her gifts and ministries. Be sensitive if he or she does not desire an active role in the ministry of the church. You may lose a qualified pastor if you do not include the spouse in the search process.

Moving from Stage to Stage

You will need to make a decision on how to manage the process of moving pastors from stage to stage. There are two basic options to consider.

1. You can choose to work with each pastor, as he or she becomes known to you. This will result in your dealing with pastors at different stages at the same time. You may be at the interview stage with four, reviewing pastoral questionnaires of another five, have eight church information packets sent out waiting for responses, and have six inquiry letters in process. In this manner, you narrow the field as you move along. New pastors can be introduced at any time. However, if you feel positive about a new person at a later point in your search, you will have to try to bring him or her up to speed with others who are already more familiar to you.
2. You can study pastors' profiles as you receive them, screening a large selection of pastors before taking further action. Once a large number of profiles are reviewed, move to the next stage and then to the next, narrowing the field down as you move along in the process. In this option you may easily review 50 profiles in order to narrow the field down to 10 for overall consideration. Unless you know that all 10 candidates are open to a search inquiry, your list of 10 may easily be reduced to five or six.

There are five stages that you will move pastors through as you work with them in the search process. In each stage are specific events that must be completed before moving on to the next stage.

*   Stage I: Sharing and Gathering Information
*   Stage II: Pastoral Profile and Questionnaire
*   Stage III: Sermon Tapes, Reference Checks, and Testing
*   Stage IV: Interviews
*   Stage V: Determining Whom to Recommend

In order to know where any one pastor is at any given time in your search process, you need to create a tracking file. This may be done on paper in a binder or via a computer printout, but it must be done. At each search committee meeting, the members need to receive an updated copy of the chart. Mark new or changed entries with an asterisk or print them in bold type so that changes can be easily seen. A sample chart can be found on page 56.

At any stage, if a pastor and/or the search committee decide not to continue further communications, move the name and information to a *dropped* stage in your tracking file. You need to remember all the pastors with whom you communicated; some may indicate being open for additional correspondence or reconsideration at a later date. Some pastors may find that their current church situation has changed, or that they are no longer talking with another church about a call, or that they have had a change of heart and thus are open to beginning a dialogue with you about your church.

Stage I: Sharing and Gathering Information

Your initial contact is an inquiry. The pastor has been sent an inquiry letter or was contacted by telephone. The pastor is added to your tracking file at this point. If your initial introduction to a candidate is the result of reviewing a pastor's profile received from your denomination, and if you decide not to make personal contact with that candidate, still add the pastor's name to your tracking file. That pastor may decide to contact you independently, and you need to know that he or she has already been reviewed. Knowing whom you have reviewed is important for both you and them and can save time for all parties.

Some pastors will not have profiles, or their profiles will be out of date. You might, if your denominational polity permits, simply choose to contact some people directly. The first sample letter below, with a copy of your ad if one is used, may be sent for an initial direct contact. In your initial letter of inquiry, if you give a date when a search committee member will telephone, be sure that the phone call is made on the given date.

Greetings from Anytown Community Church!

Anytown Community Church is currently seeking a pastor. You have been suggested as a possible candidate, and we would like to know if you are open to further discussion regarding a call at this time.

We are looking for a Spirit-filled man or woman who is excited about ministering to God's people and together reaching out to the community.

A copy of our recent ad is enclosed. We have prepared a comprehensive information package about our church and its ministries that will be sent to pastors who are interested in hearing more about us. The package is sent upon receipt of a pastoral profile, providing our search committee believes there is a possibility of a good match between you and us.

A committee member will be calling you on _____ [*give a date 10 days out*] to inquire about your interest in Anytown Community Church. We are dedicated to being proactive in all areas of communication in our pastoral search and to do a high-quality search for all parties involved.

We are looking forward to talking with you.

This stage continues when the search committee receives a query back from an interested pastor. Based on this positive initial response, you may send out your church information packet, including your pastoral questionnaire. You may also send a packet in response to a reply to an ad or inquiry letter. Record in your tracking file the date the packet was sent. The search committee must decide whether or not to send any packets to pastors before receiving and reviewing their profiles. Once the packet is sent, you will need to follow up with a phone call within 10 days to two weeks to answer any questions and to determine if further communications are warranted.

Once the packet has been sent and if the pastor is open to further communication, he or she should be encouraged to complete your pastoral questionnaire found in the packet. If you do not have a copy of his or her pastoral profile, request a copy at this time.

Stage II: Pastoral Profile and Questionnaire

Once the pastoral profile and questionnaire are received, make copies for the search committee members to review prior to your next meeting. The pastoral profile is discussed in the chapter "Finding Candidates." A sample pastoral questionnaire form can be found in appendix B.

You can learn a great deal about a candidate from a pastoral profile. The form will provide information about a pastor's personal history, his or her ministry and professional preferences, and leadership and management style. This information will help you understand who the pastor is and what type of ministry he or she is searching for. You may be interested in a pastor but find that he or she is interested in a rural ministry, and you are a metropolitan, inner-city ministry. Your church may have a vibrant youth and singles ministry, and a possible candidate indicates he or she does not work well with youth. These two pastors would likely be eliminated from your list. On the other hand, a pastor who indicates an interest in outreach might do well in your church if you have a thriving evangelistic ministry. Read the profiles carefully.

The pastoral questionnaire will provide the search committee with insights beyond what the pastoral profile shows. You can ask questions that you consider to be relevant to your church, leadership, and congregation, and that will help you learn more about each pastor's style in leadership, administration, worship, education, evangelism, and fellowship. Each pastor needs to complete the same questionnaire. The sample questionnaire was developed after consultation with pastors. It is non-threatening and simply asks for a response to key words or phrases, allowing the pastor to complete it in a short period of time. You will receive short and concise statements in response. If you have identified issues that are important to your church and you need to know how each pastor feels about them, include questions about them in your questionnaire. The responses each pastor provides must be matched against what you determine is appropriate for your church and ministry. Whether you use this questionnaire, modify it for your church's needs, or use another, remember that the pastor still has a church to minister to and cannot take hours completing a long form.

As the search committee discusses the pastoral profile and questionnaire, committee members need to be aware of what will affect their decisions. The chapter "Selection Criteria, Evaluation, and Recommendation" provides guidelines on establishing a method of assessing pastoral candidates.

Stage III: Sermon Tapes, Reference Checks, and Testing

With a positive decision on the questionnaire and profile, several events can now happen at the same time. Call the pastor and request an audiotape or videotape of a recent complete worship service. If the candidate's church does not tape services, ask if an exception could be made. Sermon tapes are valuable instruments in the search process and help committee members connect with the pastor. A tape of a sermon without the complete service is harder to evaluate, so request one that contains the whole service.

An audiotape is sufficient, yet a videotape has advantages since you can observe the pastor as worship leader and get a better feel for the flow of the service. When the tape is received, make copies for each member of the search committee. An audiotape can be evaluated on application, Biblical content, challenge, delivery, humor, illustrations, worship flow, celebratory worship, prayer, and sermon length. Videotapes can also be evaluated on the same criteria plus charisma, eye contact, comfortableness, mannerisms, movement, personality, and appearance. Talk about the tapes as a committee, deciding on your individual and combined reactions. You might want to request tapes from two separate worship services. These will provide a better picture of the candidate's worship style and messages. For more specifics on evaluating preaching and the worship service, review the section called "The Importance of Preaching" in the chapter "Selection Criteria, Evaluation, and Recommendation."

Decide whether or not the search committee budget allows travel to hear pastors. Some committees may feel the benefits of observing a worship service far outweigh the expense. Actually observing a worship service conducted by a pastoral candidate is recommended if geographically possible. If visiting to observe a Sunday service, decide beforehand if you will let the pastor know you will be there.

While waiting for the tape, begin your reference checks. If you choose to do personality testing, that process needs to start. See the sections called "Reference Checks" and "Test Instruments" in the chapter "Managing References, Testing, Interviews, and Red Flags" for guidelines on these processes. When the checks have been completed and the search committee feels good about continuing, move on to the next stage.

Stage IV: Interviews

Now is the time to contact the pastor to arrange an interview. If the pastor is close by, the interview can be done face-to-face. If the distance is great, arrange for an interview via a telephone conference call. Let the pastor know when the search committee meets, and ask if he or she could be available at that time. Work your interview around his or her schedule. See "The Interview" section in the chapter "Managing References, Testing, Interviews and Red Flags" for guidelines on interviewing. This important stage is usually the first time the combined team has an opportunity to talk with the pastor. You know the candidate from the profile and questionnaire, and the candidate knows you from your church information packet. The interview is the opportunity to get to know each other at a deeper level.

Stage V: Determining Whom to Recommend

When the pastoral profiles have been read, reference checks made, tapes reviewed, interviews completed, and the personality testing is in progress, the field will begin to narrow. Talk candidly about each pastor and his or her potential fit for your church's strengths and weaknesses, character and personality, ministries, and vision and mission. Some pastors will be eliminated by their own choosing, accepting another call, deciding that they are not a good match for your church, or simply deciding to stay where they are currently serving. See the chapter "Selection Criteria, Evaluation, and Recommendation" for guidelines on this part of the process.

This phase can be very difficult. Allow each member to talk openly and without interruption about each pastor being considered. Doubts must be shared within the committee and openly discussed. Whether you vote formally or simply come to an agreement, there should be consensus among the committee that the decision is right for both your church and the pastor being considered. Following this discussion, rank your top choices and move forward with the invitations for the pastors to come for a weekend with your congregation.

In some churches, the search committee chooses the candidate and recommends that person to the board and the congregation for a call. Other churches select two candidates and present them both for the congregation to consider. Whether to present one, two, or even more is a matter of the pastoral field you have to work with, the personal choices of the search committee, and your denomination's church order or policies. Two candidates are easier to work with than three and simpler for the congregation to deal with. It is easier to host two pastors on back-to-back weekends and then make a decision than to have three pastors come out over three weekends. With a trio, the first pastor may not receive as fair an evaluation as the third. Selecting from a trio of candidates is also harder because the addition of a third pastor may make it more difficult to obtain a consensus regarding which of the three will be issued a final call. The decision about how many pastors will be recommended should be made early in the search process. See the chapter "Managing the Call Process" for guidelines on this part of the process.

If you received an inquiry from a pastor, or if a pastor knows you have been considering him or her, you need to send a letter of explanation for dropping the pastor from consideration. The sample letter below may be used as a guide. If there was no personal contact with the pastor, you need not send a letter. You do not need to keep your denominational or regional offices informed about your decisions unless specifically requested.

Our Pastoral Search Committee would like to thank you for your interest in Anytown Community Church. We appreciate your response to our ad.

Much of our initial process has been to reflect on our past, identify our strengths and weaknesses, and assess our vision and goals. Through this process, we have determined specific areas of pastoral gifts that we feel are needed at this time to guide our church. Much of this is based on the leadership styles and gifts of our previous pastors who have shaped the congregation and the direction toward which we as a congregation are moving. We have considered many qualified pastors. In reviewing your profile and our questionnaire against our church's profile, and after praying for direction, we believe we would not be a good match for you at this time.

Your profile reflects positive experiences and gifts that we know will be a benefit to a church that matches your profile. As we pray for God's guidance to our search process, we also will pray for God to bless your present and future ministry.

Tracking Pastors

The secretary of the search committee needs to track contacts and actions with each pastor. The easiest method is to attach a list of steps to the first page of each pastor's profile. It is better to be too thorough than to miss an important contact or event. Dates can be added to the list as steps are completed.

Inquiry letter sent _____

Interest (yes/no/maybe later) _____

Church information packet sent _____

Follow-up call made   _____
Pastoral profile received: current (yes/no)   _____
    New profile requested   _____
    Profile received   _____
Pastoral profile reviewed   _____
Questionnaire received   _____
Questionnaire reviewed   _____
Sermon audio- or videotape requested   _____
Sermon audio- or videotape reviewed   _____
References checked   _____
Testing completed/reviewed   _____
Telephone interview completed   _____
Disposition:
    Advance to final stage   _____
    Do not pursue   _____
    Notification of decision sent   _____
    Materials returned   _____
    Church packet returned   _____

It is helpful for the search committee to know where in the search process each prospective candidate is. The chart on pages 56 and 57 provides that type of tracking, taking each pastor through the different stages. Track the dates when the initial inquiry is made, when profiles and questionnaires are received, tapes received, reference checks made, testing reviewed, and the interview completed. Move the names from section to section as they progress though the process. Be sure to move the dropped names to the last section in order to know whom you have contacted. Some pastors may indicate they could be open to further discussion at a later date if you are still in the search process. Remove profiles from your binder when their status changes to "not available" or "dropped," but retain all profiles until the search process is completed.

Use this as a guide to developing your own tracking system. Make yours as simple or complex as you feel is necessary to provide the information to your search committee about the status of each pastor in your process.

Communication is a large part of your search effort. At every point in the search process there will be some type of communication with pastors. You need to do it well. As you move forward, you will be working on several aspects of the process at the same time. "Managing References, Testing, Interviews, and Red Flags" is explained in chapter 7. It is necessary to also review chapter 8, "Selection Criteria, Evaluation, and Recommendation," in order to know how to assess each pastor. Some of the committee members should be looking at chapter 9, "Presenting Your Best Side," while others should begin studying "Managing the Call Process," chapter 10. It may sound overwhelming, but when you understand the process, all the pieces of the puzzle fall into place.

Prospective Candidates

	Church location	Inquiry (I) Packet (P) Both (B)	Profile (P) Quest (Q) Both (B)	Sermon tape reviewed	References checked	Testing done	Interview completed
Stage V: Determining Whom to Recommend							
Pastor 4	Orange, CA	9-21 (B)	9-28 (B)	10-20	11-12	11-28	12-16
Pastor 11	Ames, IA	10-22 (B)	10-29 (B)	11-15	11-20	12-6	12-14
Stage IV: Interviews							
Pastor 8	Trenton, NJ	10-16 (B)	10-30 (B)	11-16	11-24	12-2	12-14
Pastor 9	Wichita, KS	10-20 (B)	11-8 (B)	11-20	11-26	12-8	12-16
Stage III: Sermon Tapes, Reference Checks, and Testing							
Pastor 3	Buffalo, NY	9-26 (B)	10-8 (B)	10-29	11-16		
Pastor 7	Prescott, AZ	10-6 (B)	11-2 (B)	11-26			

Stage II: Pastoral Profile and Questionnaire

Pastor 5	Pueblo, CO	9-29 (B)	10-26 (Q)		
Pastor 10	Bend, OR	10-18 (B)	11-13 (P)		

Stage I: Sharing and Information Gathering

Pastor 2	Marion, OH	9-26 (P)			
Pastor 13	Reno, NV	11-16 (I)			
Pastor 14	Minneapolis, MN	12-10 (I)			

Dropped

Pastor 1	Atlanta, GA	9-10	9-15		Not a match
Pastor 6	Seattle, WA	9-29	10-20	11-6	Not a match
Pastor 12	York, PA				No interest

Task Cluster:
Communications with Pastors

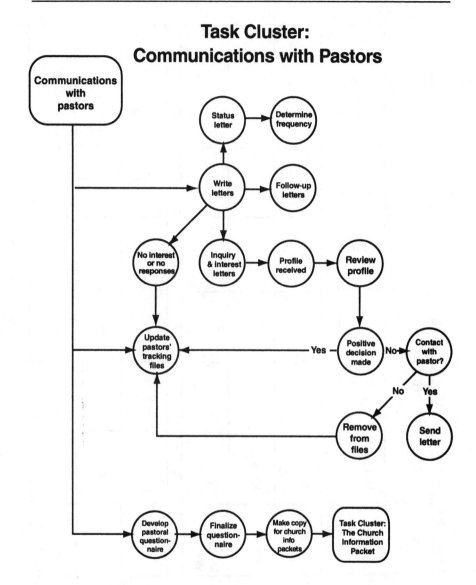

Task Cluster:
Moving from Stage to Stage

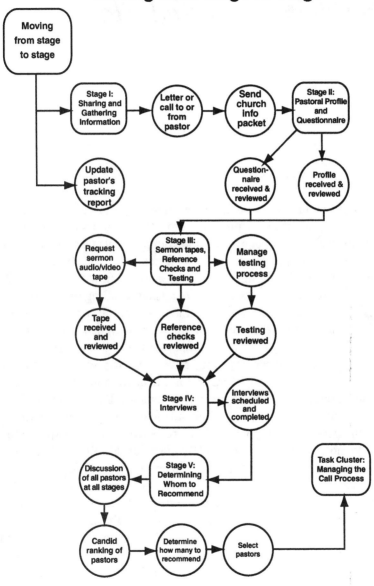

CHAPTER 7

Managing References, Testing, Interviews, and Red Flags

Checking References

A candidate should provide three or more references. These may be requested on the pastoral profile forms that you receive from your denominational or regional offices or in your pastoral questionnaire. These are individuals whom the search committee may ask about a pastor's abilities and gifts for ministry. Let the pastor know that you will be checking references. You should feel okay about calling these individuals and asking questions. It works best to have one search committee member make calls to all the references for one pastor. When calling, identify yourself, your church, and the purpose for the call. Ask if the time is convenient and if he or she has 10 to 15 minutes to answer a few questions about pastor "x." If not, make an appointment for another time. Explain that you are interested in short, concise statements. Remember to take into consideration the time zones if calling out of your area. Do not ask for a call back if the person is out; you should be responsible for the expense of the call. Take notes during or immediately after the call. Remember that you are responsible for giving the full search committee a report on the calls.

Be candid in your conversation. If you sense hesitancy, ask for clarification. Emphasize that all comments will be kept in confidence and will be shared only with the search committee. At the end of each call, ask if there are any final thoughts the person would like to share. Finally, thank each person for his or her assistance. If several of the references are not available when you try to make contact, request others from the pastor.

Prepare a short list of questions before making the call. Again, emphasize that the information will be kept in confidence. Below are sample questions.

- How long have you known Pastor _____?
- What ministry relationships have you had with Pastor _____?
- Can you state Pastor _____'s vision?
- How does Pastor _____ lead his/her congregation?
- How does Pastor _____ develop personal growth in his/her ministry?
- How does Pastor _____ challenge the congregation?
- Please describe what area of Pastor _____'s ministry is his/her greatest strength and ability.
- Are there any areas of Pastor _____'s ministry that could benefit from development and attention?
- How do you feel about Pastor _____'s credibility?
- Do you have any other candid and confidential comments you would like to share?

As references are checked, the search committee may sense an issue or question that needs additional explanation. Further clarification may resolve your questions. Call back the person with whom you first spoke. To clarify any questions, you might also contact other references, pastors in the region or denomination, or even the candidate. Do your best to resolve the question.

Using Test Instruments

One of the means to determine whether a pastor would be a good match for your church is to use one of the many test instruments available through a Christian counselor or a Christian management consultant. This form of testing has become acceptable in churches, seminaries, and mission fields across the country. Available tests include the Taylor-Johnson Temperament Analysis and the Myers-Briggs Type Indicator. The counselor might recommend others, based on his or her knowledge and training. These tests identify areas of leadership and personality styles, communication and team style and skills, and temperaments. The tests can effectively identify areas of *match* between the pastor and the church. The use of two tests is recommended for a check and balance. The management of the tests by an experienced counselor is important. Do not pick a test simply because you have heard of it. Choose a test based on the recommendations of the counselor only after meeting with him or her. The counselor's knowledge of the testing instrument, especially how to score and interpret it, is the key to having the tests help the search process. Try not to pick a test or tests that take more than one hour to complete.

Look in the telephone book listings under "Counselors" or "Marriage, Family, Child, and Individual Counselors." Your first preference should naturally be a Christian counselor, but be aware that not all counselors who are committed Christians identify themselves as such in the telephone book or other directories or promotional material. Contact pastors from neighboring churches and ask for names of counselors with whom they have worked. Call several counselors and ask whether they do psychological testing and evaluation and if they have experience using tests in pastoral searches. Then invite one to come and talk to your search committee. This meeting is an important starting point for the counselor. Information you provide about your church and its staff, board, and members will help the counselor understand who you are. He or she needs to know the type of leader you are looking for, characteristics sought, and something about your church. You may be asked about your previous pastor. When a counselor knows what it is you hope to gain through testing, appropriate test instruments can be recommended. If there is not a Christian counselor in your area, the process can be done via mail and conference calls between the search committee and the counselor.

What will be determined in the testing process is why one pastor would be a better match for your church than another pastor. Your search committee is called to discover the pastor that God would have serve your church, so it is important to discover the pastor who will be the best match for your church.

The counselor will provide the search committee and each pastor with an identical, written summary of the test(s). The summary should address the matter of an appropriate match for the pastor and the church, not point out deficiency issues or problem areas. The summary content will be based on the test used. Costs will vary based on the number and type of test(s) used.

The sample letter below can be used to introduce the testing process to the pastor. Not all pastors will appreciate your using these tests. Some may even elect not to complete the tests, but the majority will appreciate the opportunity to find out more about themselves. In fairness, if you decide to use the tests, *all* pastors should have to complete them in order to be considered.

Our pastoral search committee is moving forward in our search process and we are excited about the men and women with whom we are communicating. We have completed communications with the references provided, listened to worship tapes, and are moving into the next stages of the process.

As stated in an earlier phone call, we have arranged with Christian Counseling Center, Inc. (CCC) to send one test to all pastors we are considering. The Taylor-Johnson Temperament Analysis focuses on general personality characteristics to identify a match with our style and ministry requirements. The test instrument will be administered by Bill Fielding of CCC who will send the test with an explanatory cover letter, score it, and give us a summary of findings that he feels will assist us in our search process. He will also send you the same summary of findings. He alone will see and handle the test, so your confidentiality will be protected. You should receive the material in a few days.

It is our prayer that the test or the test process will not offend you. Most churches today use some form of tests in their search process. Additionally, many seminaries use tests with new students, and placements into selected ministry areas often require testing. We selected a test that will not be too time-consuming or threatening, and we feel this test can benefit both you and our church by ensuring a good match.

We hope you can find an hour to do the test as soon as possible. We realize time is valuable but would appreciate your completing the test in the coming week.

We have heard good things about you as a pastor and pray for God's best for you in your ministry search. Should you have any questions about Anytown Community Church, our ministries, or our search process, please call.

The testing process is a subject that should be kept confidential between the search committee and the pastors. There is no need for the congregation to know about it.

The Interview

The interview provides an opportunity for direct interaction between the full search committee and the pastor being considered. This may be by telephone or face-to-face. The search committee chairperson needs to phone the pastor and arrange an interview at a time convenient for all parties. Let him or her know how much time to plan on and what time you will call. If the pastor is married, invite his or her spouse to join in a portion of the conversation. When scheduling two calls for the same evening, allow time between the two to review the first interview before moving into the second. The entire search committee should be present at all interviews.

Allow one-half hour for the call. All committee members should have reviewed their copies of the pastor's profile and pastoral questionnaire prior to the call. Decide who will lead off the questions and watch your time closely. One person should be in charge of the conversation. Let each committee member ask at least two questions. A list of potential questions as well as possible questions you should be prepared to answer is included below. Develop more questions based on the pastor's profile and pastoral questionnaire, your church structure, and your strengths and weaknesses. Ask yourselves, "What questions are still lingering in my mind about this person?" Allow time for the pastor to ask any final questions. Before ending the call, let him or her know what happens next. Let them know when and how soon will you make contact. Committee members should take notes during and after the call, recording enough information about the call to be able to reflect on the interview at a later date when the field is being narrowed down. Each member should note significant impressions.

If you do not have access to a telephone with a speakerphone, consider purchasing one at a cost of about $30. With permission from the pastor, consider taping the calls for listening to later when the process is further along.

Before the phone call is made, each committee member should think about questions that he or she would like to ask. Below are some sample questions. Talk about these as a group so that questions are not duplicated.

- What is your passion?
- Tell us about your call to ministry.
- How do you achieve personal growth in your ministry?
- How do you challenge the congregation?

- What style of worship do you enjoy?
- What expectations do you have of the board?
- What expectations do you have of the congregation?
- What situations frustrate you the most?
- Describe your areas of greatest strength and ability.
- How do you handle leadership training?
- When facing a problem, what questions do you naturally ask?
- What is your leadership style?
- How will you know God's will in this matter?

In preparing for the interview, remember that you also will be asked questions. Below are several questions you might be asked.

- Why are you interested in me as a pastor?
- What role do you expect my family to have in your church?
- What concerns need to be addressed in the congregation and the community?
- What significant events and people have shaped your church, and how?
- What is your vision for your congregation?

Dealing with Red Flags

As you read pastors' profiles and their pastoral questionnaires, listen to their sermon tapes, interview them, or talk to their references, there may be pastors about whom search committee members feel some uncertainty. Call these uncertainties *red flags* and allow them to be discussed in your meetings.

It is wise to understand from the start that not every pastor will be a good match for your church, and some of them will not seem right because of these red flags. Each member of the search committee has the obligation to raise any red-flag issues, when they sense them, to the committee. The committee then needs to discuss the issue and find answers to the questions. That may mean talking to the pastor or to his or her references, asking for more references, talking to a regional pastor where the pastor is serving, or simply talking as a committee. After you have researched the issue, make your decision. Some red flags will close a relationship. If this is the case and you have been in conversation with the pastor, a letter or phone call should be made soon to let the pastor know the committee has decided he or she is not a good match for the congregation.

Red flags may take many forms. It may be as simple as a strong feeling that several search committee members have about a pastor. It may be because the candidate's views on a topic are different from those of the majority of your church membership. You may sense that the pastor might not relate to a specific age group in your church that you see as a priority. It may be about worship style, sermon delivery, or even a control issue. If the red flag is one about relationships, probe deeply, contacting people who can clarify your questions. Whatever the issue, the search committee needs to talk it through and make a decision. Remember that there are two sides to every issue, so take the time to respectfully explore both sides.

The process of checking references, testing, conducting interviews, and dealing with red flags can be time-consuming. Whether you are working with three pastors or six pastors in this phase of the search process, you will be busy. There are many phone calls to make and reports to read. Your search is narrowing down. The rewards will be great as you continue in the search process and determine your selection criteria, evaluate each pastor, and finally, make a recommendation.

Task Cluster: Managing References, Testing, Interviews, and Red Flags

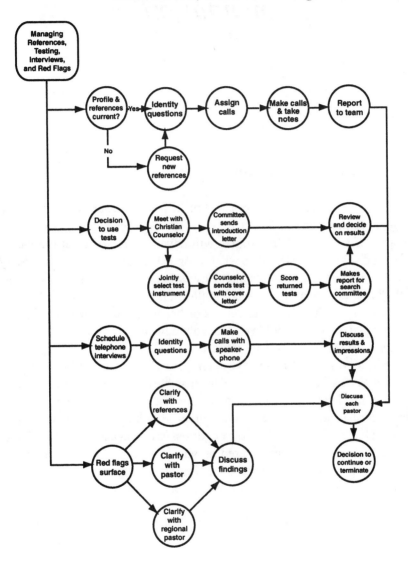

Selection Criteria, Evaluation, and Recommendation

Identifying Your Selection Criteria

It is important to determine the selection criteria for your pastoral search. A good starting point is to talk about your vision of a new pastor. Each member of your search committee will have a vision of what the pastor could and should be, as well as what he or she should not be. You already know what your church looks like. Now, what would it look like with this pastor? Spend time as a search committee talking about this area. What is your vision of your church under his or her leadership? What skills and professional qualities would you like your new pastor to have? What types of experience or education are important?

A second step is to identify specific attributes that you find valuable in a new pastor. Below is a list of many possible attributes. Use this list, add to it, or develop your own. Narrow your list down to the top 12 to 15 attributes that you as a committee agree on as important for your next pastor. Then rank them into two categories: essential and desirable. These attributes need to be remembered as you talk about each pastor in the evaluation process. The list can be an important resource to share with a Christian counselor if you decide to use personality tests.

Aggressive	Responsible	People-person	Persistent
Approachable	Dedicated	Empathic	Insightful
Caring	Assertive	Takes the initiative	Tolerant
Called/committed	Friendly	Supportive	Delegates
Humorous	Analytical	Program facilitator	Trustworthy
Conflict resolver	Unifier	Persuasive	Discreet
Administrator	Communicator	Trainer	Organized

Sensitive	Problem solver	Studious	Flexible
Goal setter	Positive	Planner	Strong
Traditionalist	Loyal	Perceptive	Progressive
Positive self-image	Mature	Good listener	Disciplined
Personal integrity	Effective	Enthusiastic	Professional
Stable	Team player	Precise	Imaginative
Humility	Intuitive	Innovative	Honest
Intelligent	Determined	Energetic	Reliable
Creative	Results-oriented	Diligent	Diplomatic

As you read pastors' profiles and their pastoral questionnaires and talk to pastors and their references, use your intuition to determine if the pastor has the attributes you selected.

The third step is to review your completed congregational survey. The survey you used has areas that will help you in determining your selection criteria. The sample congregational survey in appendix A has several areas. It first asks the congregation to identify important professional qualities of and expectations for the new pastor. Some specific items are preaching, administration, leadership, counseling, and program development. It then asks about congregational strengths, weaknesses, needs, and interests. Specific items include ministries to youth or seniors, community outreach, education, family ministries, worship services, and discipleship. The results of your survey will tell you how the congregation thinks about key pastoral and congregational areas. If you have recently completed strategic planning or a master plan of your church, review that document for similar information.

Weighing of Selection Criteria

Did the congregation identify some of the same desired professional qualities as you did? Did the results of your survey match what the search committee thought were the congregational strengths, weaknesses, needs, and issues? Did the results of your survey match the vision the search committee has of your new pastor? What pastoral skills and background are necessary to work well with the strengths, weaknesses, needs, and interests of your congregation? Talk about these questions to finalize your selection criteria.

Having identified your selection criteria, list them by three categories:

1) preferred skills and background, 2) desired personal attributes, and 3) areas of congregational focus. Keep your list as concise as possible. After developing your list of criteria by category, talk about them as a committee. Which are the most important? Which are secondary? Decide what weight value you would put on each category. It might be helpful to use a fraction or percentage value to weigh each category. Are the pastor's skills and background worth 50 percent of your criteria or should they be worth more? If you choose 50 percent as a value for skills and background, with 25 percent as a value for personal attributes and 25 percent as a value for your congregation's focus, then each pastor you consider should be gauged against these same percentages. If you decide that all three cate-gories are equally important, then each category will be worth one-third. In any case, every pastor should be evaluated against 100 percent of your selection criteria. Determine what the minimum acceptable criteria are.

A thorough knowledge of your selection criteria can help you when reviewing and discussing pastoral questionnaires and when participating in interviews. As you read pastors' questionnaires, listen to their worship tapes, and finally interview them, you will be better able to relate their experiences, skills, and personal qualities to what you have identified as important selection criteria. Using your intuition is valuable in moving forward in the selection process, and an established set of selection criteria will help you feel comfortable with your intuition.

The Importance of Preaching

The search committee needs to talk about the importance of preaching and leading worship and come to a decision on how they will rank this in relation to all other selection criteria.

The decision to consider a pastor should not be based on preaching alone but needs to take into account other professional skills and gifts. Administration, leadership, planning and vision setting, team building, and other areas of ministries are important. However, the bottom line is usually that preaching and leading worship tend to stand out as deciding factors.

Whatever professional skills and gifts you determine to be your selection criteria, a basic fact remains. If the preaching is weak, the church may suffer. The congregation sees and hears more of a pastor in the pulpit than in any other role. He or she may be the best administrator in the world, but if the preaching is dull or the messages weak, other areas of ministry will suffer. This is truer in one-pastor churches than in churches where other staff may share in the preaching and other ministry areas. Talk as a committee about how the church can grow with good preaching and about how lives will be changed and members challenged as God's Word lives in them. But be careful that your expectations about the results of the pastor's preaching are realistic.

How can the search committee know good preaching? Based on their own experiences, all members will have preconceived ideas about what good preaching is. It is helpful for the committee to understand generally accepted criteria for good preaching.

On pages 23 and 24 of her book, *So You're Looking for a New Preacher*, Elizabeth Achtemeier distills her wisdom learned as an adjunct professor of Bible and homiletics. She states, "In short, good preaching leads you into a new or renewed experience of the work of God in your life and in the life of your congregation. Good preaching opens the way for God's action and God's changes to be wrought in human hearts and lives." She makes specific recommendations about understanding preaching and worship.

- Weigh the message against the Word. Is the pastor's message from the Word and illuminated by Scripture?
- Do the illustrations and language make the message clear?
- Are we reminded that God is active here and now in our lives?
- Is the structure of the message logical? Can you trace its argument?
- Does the message hold your interest to its end and appeal to your heart as well as your mind?
- Are the prayers, music, and other parts of the liturgy connected with the message?
- Are the prayers to God or to the congregation? Do they express sincere offerings of heartfelt praise and confession, petition, and gratitude?
- Does the message and the delivery carry a sense of energy?
- Does the pastor seem to be worshiping with the congregation?
- What attitude is conveyed by the pastor's delivery–his or her voice, gestures, and body language?

Achtemeier also recommends learning about the pastor's personal life and growth areas.

- Ask how he or she is growing in an understanding of Scripture. What are his or her disciplines of Bible study and prayer?
- Ask about personal study habits. What theology books has the pastor read in the last three months?
- Ask about other literature. What has the pastor recently read that develops his or her imagination, creativity, and style of speech?
- Ask about other interests. What does the pastor do in his or her spare time?
- Ask about the pastor's commitment to continuing education. What would he or she do with five to ten days of study leave per year?

The Evaluation Process

From the time of the initial contact with each pastor, you will be in an evaluation mode. The first piece of information you will see about most pastors will either be the pastoral profile or the pastoral questionnaire. As these are read and discussed in your meetings, you will need to make a decision about whether or not to move forward in the process with each pastor. In some cases the answer will be very clear to all committee members, while at other times you will have to talk quite a while before deciding. You may also decide to continue to the next stage in the process to gain additional information before making a decision.

Each piece of information will provide more data on which to base your decision. From the pastoral profile, move to a completed pastoral questionnaire. From the pastoral questionnaire, move to the calls made to the references. From the reference calls, move to the worship tape with a sermon. From the tape, move to the personal interview. There may also be calls to the pastor, in addition to the interview, that may provide more information. If you talk to other pastors, regional pastors, or denominational representatives, take their views into account.

In the early stages of the search process you evaluated pastors based on the information they provided. As you narrow the field, your evaluations of the remaining pastors will become more focused. In addition to how well each pastor meets your selection criteria, there are other important factors that will influence your evaluation.

- The results of test instruments and feedback from the counselor
- Your personal interview with the pastor

- The comments from your reference checks
- The sermon and worship tape
- The pastoral questionnaire
- The pastoral profile

As you talk about each of these factors, pieces of the puzzle will fit together. The information you receive about each pastor, piece by piece, will serve to build a picture in each of your minds about him or her. Discuss each pastor candidly.

- How does he or she rank against your selection criteria?
- How do you rate the preaching and worship?
- What were the comments from the references?
- Do the test instruments suggest a good match?
- Did the pastor's answers on the pastoral questionnaire help you understand him or her and seem to be what your church needs?
- Were you strongly influenced by the personal interview?
- How well do you think the pastor will work with other staff, and vice versa?

Take time at your meetings to review your findings. Ask each other, "If we were to choose now, whom would we choose and why?" Some members may have insights that others miss. You will be surprised at how often you find you are not that far apart in your thoughts. With the information received, you will need to make a decision at some point with each pastor whom you consider. Whether you have looked at two pastors or 50 pastors, you will be making decisions based on information known at that point. This evaluation process will continue up to the final vote on which pastor to call. You will pass over some pastors in this process and the field will narrow automatically. When pastors are dropped from consideration, each should receive a letter as soon as possible. Some pastors will likewise choose to pass over you and will eliminate themselves from consideration.

Making Your Recommendation

After your evaluation is complete, you will need to make a recommendation to your board about which pastor(s) to invite for final consideration. This recommendation needs to be based on which pastor(s) the committee thinks will make the best match for your congregation and ministries. You could recommend one pastor. Some search committees recommend presenting two pastors from which the congregation may choose. There are cases of three pastors being offered to congregations, but this can be very confusing to the congregation. The committee must be aware of denominational or regional rules that affect their decision.

If you have five pastors at the final stage, you need to make choices based on your combined knowledge of all the information received and the results of your evaluation process. The committee's presentation to the board should establish the credibility of the selected pastor(s), the committee's reasons for selecting each pastor, and how each one will meet the identified needs of the church. If you have kept the board members informed about your process and about the pastors you are considering, they will most likely concur. Once the recommendation is approved, move to the chapter on "Managing the Call Process."

Nontraditional Recommendations

Calling Seminary Candidates

Seminary candidates who have met the course and field requirements are often eligible for call after the appropriate seminary or denominational bodies have approved them. Their candidacy is often announced in the appropriate denominational medium. Candidates who have trained in theological seminaries other than those approved by your denomination must usually meet requirements identified by your denomination. Investigate whether your denomination has specific guidelines for considering and calling seminary candidates.

In some denominations, names of all pastors and seminarians are made available through judicatory channels. But in other denominations, names of seminary candidates are available through theological seminaries. If you wish to consider a student, you would contact the seminary of your choice in winter for names of students graduating at the end of the following school year. Usually a specific individual or office is responsible for placement.

Calling Pastors of Other Denominations

In the course of the search process, you may receive an inquiry from a pastor or know of a pastor who interests you, yet this person is in another denomination. If the pastoral profile interests you and you want to move him or her into your full search process, you must consider the constraints placed upon you by your denomination. These cases must be managed with extra care and attention to detail. Contact your denominational or regional offices for their assistance.

Initially, you will work with a pastor from another denomination in the same manner as if that candidate was from your denomination. As you move further along in the process however, you will have several additional tasks. First, your church order may contain special procedures to be followed if you decide to issue a call to him or her. Second, you should request references from the candidate's two previous congregations. Third, contact the pastor's local regional pastor or synod to determine if there were any issues or problems in previous congregations. The purpose in these last two tasks is to determine if there is a history of problems. Ask the hard questions. While unlikely, there may be occasions when a pastor will want to change denominations to leave behind a problematic history.

Some denominations will allow a pastor from another denomination to be considered only after the congregation has put forth a sustained and realistic effort to obtain a minister from within the denomination. Two other situations may allow for approaching such a pastor.

- The minister to be called has such extraordinary qualifications that it would be important for the denomination to acquire his or her services.
- The need of a particular congregation for a pastor is so urgent or the congregation's circumstances are so unusual that they can be met only by calling a minister from another denomination.

If a pastor is called from another denomination, work with your regional or denominational offices to determine what specific documentation they need to accept the pastor. The candidate may need to provide copies of a completed pastor's profile form, academic degrees and seminary transcript, and ministry references. He or she may also be required to give a statement attesting to knowledge of your denomination's history, church order, and its agencies and institutions.

Calling for a Specific Term of Service

There may be occasions when a church determines it appropriate to extend a call to a pastor for a specific term of service. This is most likely when a church has a specialized ministry. The ministry may be new with an uncertain outcome, perhaps funded for a specific period of time, or it may represent a unique opportunity with a limited time frame. If this is the case, there are several processes you should follow. First, be certain that your advertising and communications clearly state the length of the call. Second, the call letter should designate the specific term, address the possibility and method for reappointment (if applicable), and outline the financial arrangements if the appointment is not extended beyond the specified term. Third, your church supervisor or counselor should determine that the termination procedures and arrangements in your letter of call are fair and reasonable.

It takes time to agree on what selection criteria you will use to evaluate pastors. The evaluations are also difficult as your committee talks about each pastor and how each fits your church. Finding the best match for your church and your ministries is vital. Spend time in prayer and lean on God in this phase of the search process. He will lead you to a recommendation. Once a pastor has been chosen, you need to talk about the best way to present your church to the pastor and the pastor to the congregation.

Task Cluster:
Selection Criteria

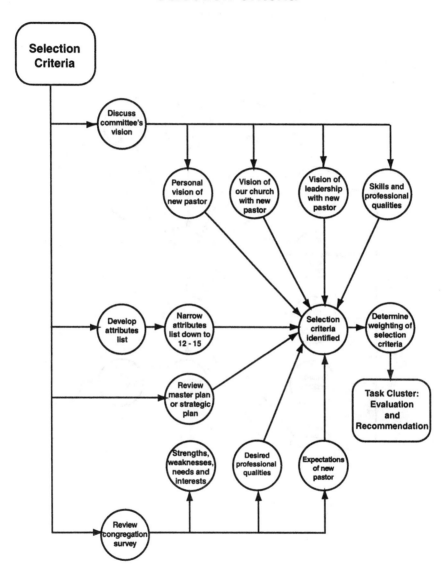

Task Cluster:
Evaluation and Recommendation

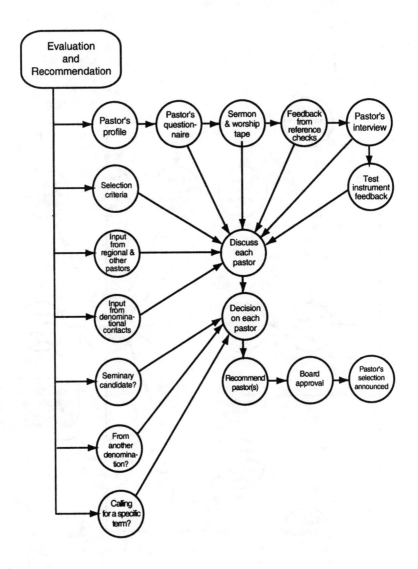

CHAPTER 9

Presenting Your Best Side

Pastors' Perspectives

How you present yourself when hosting a pastor and the materials you prepare create an impression in the pastor's mind. He or she is forming opinions of the leaders, how friendly the congregation is, and whether or not the information you gave about your church is accurate. These impressions and opinions are an important part of the decision-making process. Surveyed pastors were very clear on what influenced their decisions. Consider the following comments as you think about how to present your best side.

- "The primary factors were their clear vision, openness to change, and ongoing outreach."
- "Spend time with the board when visiting the church. Many churches tend to put 'forward-looking' people on the search committee and 'safe' people on the board. This results in tension when you arrive and find the actual picture different from what was presented."
- "Most importantly, they indicated that as a church they were willing to learn and follow my leadership."
- "They passionately pursued calling me, mobilizing the members to encourage me."
- "They let us know how they felt our gifts for ministry could be used."
- "Every church puts its best foot forward, but there are also the less involved and fringe members. Perhaps more opportunity should be given to talk to a wider cross section of the church."

Hosting the Visit

Once a recommendation about which pastor(s) to consider has been made and approved by the board, dates for visits can be decided. You need to plan what will be done and with whom. The search committee can decide on the order of the activities based on the time available. Put together a visit that will hold the interest of the pastor and spouse yet not be too tiring. Below is a sample letter with an agenda for a visit.

Our tentative agenda for your visit here is listed below. This is not cast in concrete, but we hope it will serve to provide an opportunity for us to get to know one another.

Friday, January 8
8:00 P.M.   Arrival at the Anytown airport and driven to host family or a motel

Saturday, January 9
9:00 A.M.   Breakfast meeting with the elders
1:00 P.M.   Tour of the city
6:00 P.M..   Potluck with search committee, board members, staff, and committee leaders

Sunday, January 10
9:45 A.M.   Sunday school
11:00 A.M.   Morning worship service
12:15 P.M.   Question and answer time
1:00 P.M.   Fellowship time with coffee and cake
1:45 P.M.   Search committee wrap-up
2:00 P.M.   Lunch with members of the search committee
4:30 P.M.   Departure

Your airline tickets are enclosed. Please give us a call if there are any questions or if you have any suggested changes. We are truly looking forward to your time with us and trust God to bless us all.

Custom Fit the Itinerary

It is important for the search committee, board, staff, committee leaders, and their spouses to spend time getting to know the pastor and his or her family. The majority of the visit should be with these people. An evening potluck can allow these individuals time to interact closely with the pastor and spouse. One person should facilitate the evening's interaction. Allow time for each person to tell about his or her ministry involvement in the church. Encourage the pastor and spouse to ask questions in return.

A meeting of the elders with the pastor and spouse can be helpful in answering any questions they may have about church life, leadership styles, or problem areas where healing may be needed. Ask the pastor if there are any specific ministries or activities he or she would like to know more about.

Have one individual work with the pastor to plan the worship service. Whether through an elder, a worship leader, or the church secretary, the service needs to be coordinated with the pastor in advance of his or her arrival. Ask if the pastor would like to do a children's message. Let the pastor know if the children are dismissed at a point in the service for children's church. Advise him or her of any elements in your worship service that should be included; otherwise, the service should be the pastor's to plan and lead so that his or her gifts and ministry style come through. Make the pastor aware of any available or unique worship ministries such as choir, praise teams, special instruments, drama, and puppets, and work with him or her to use one or two that fit with the message and flow of the service. Just as the service is an opportunity for the congregation to be introduced to and hear the pastor lead worship, it should allow the pastor to see any unique worship elements that your church has to offer.

When planning the visit, make the visit fit the pastor and his or her family. There may be several pastors visiting in the call process. Invite each pastor and spouse to come for a visit. Make each visit fit their family make-up, interests, and needs. If the pastor has children, allow time to see area schools and, if possible, arrange for personalized visits to tour the schools. Members of the congregation with children in the schools might be asked to assist with the tours. If the church does not own a parsonage and is willing to work with the pastor on buying a home, be sure to show different neighborhoods in the area and provide real estate ads from the local paper. When your decision has been made and a pastor has been issued a call, you may host another visit for the pastor, the pastor and spouse, or the pastor and family.

Introducing Pastors to the Congregation

How you introduce the pastors to the congregation is important. The letter "Introducing Two Candidates to the Congregation" in appendix C shows an effective method of introducing two pastors and the voting process to the congregation. A similar introduction can be attached to a profile page about each of the pastors being presented for consideration. Create your pastor's profile page from information you received on the pastoral questionnaire (shown in appendix B). Simply summarize the key questions and answers from the pastors and add a family picture and family profile. This summary allows the congregation an opportunity to get to know the pastor and his or her family before they visit. These profiles should be distributed the week before each pastor visits. A cover letter and the profiles should probably be mailed to all member households. In small congregations, the search committee members can hand out the letter and the profiles to the congregation after a worship service. Do not simply leave them in the foyer for the congregation to pick up, because many will miss them and feel left out of the process. If there are regional or denominational procedures about introducing candidates, follow them instead.

Talking about Expectations

While you are presenting your best side, hosting the pastoral candidates, getting to know them, and allowing them to be introduced to your church, its ministries, and leaders, you need to plan time to talk about the pastor's and your expectations of each other. Through your analysis, self-study, and identification of issues done earlier in the search process, you took the first steps towards ensuring a potentially good match with a new pastor. Now, as you meet face-to-face, you have the opportunity to clarify your expectations of them and their expectations of your board and congregation. These expectations could be about ministry styles, leadership style or involvement, vision, or worship styles, to name a few areas of concern. If your church has strong feelings on specific issues, such as women holding elected office, it would be best for all concerned if these are addressed in early communications. If they have not been discussed, however, they definitely need to be discussed now. Your willingness to be candid with pastoral candidates can help avoid problems that could later lead to pastor-church conflicts.

Little Things Make a Difference

Doing some basic things can make a good impression. You should get the airline tickets and send them to the pastor, based on his or her schedule and needs. A member should meet the pastor and spouse at the gate. You should plan on picking up all the expenses related to the visits. When calls are necessary, you should make the call and incur the expense. If the pastor prefers, house the pastor and family at a member's home if at all possible. The value of fellowship and the beginning of friendships established through staying in a member's home cannot be underestimated. Be sensitive, however, to the fact that the interview process can be very draining, and some pastors might prefer the privacy and emotional space afforded by a motel. The chance to take a break might allow the pastor to feel fresh and focused during the interview, the worship service, and social events. If you do use a motel, choose a quality one.

Allow time for the pastor to visit with the elders and be sure to invite the spouse to take part. Arrange for selected members to host meals when appropriate. To give a great overview of the area, take a local map and use pins or stickers to mark the locations of the church, schools, and the homes of as many church families as possible. Before the pastor leaves, have the search committee chairperson, secretary, and their spouses take the pastor and spouse to lunch.

Presenting yourself in the best light also means looking at the church facilities and the parsonage. When the search process begins, another group might be formed to do maintenance work that has been put off in the church and the parsonage. They need to look attractive.

Building a Compensation Package

The board, through the deacons or a finance committee, needs to develop a compensation package. While it may not be actively involved in this work, the search committee needs to be certain the package is developed and ready for final approval once it has made a decision on which pastor(s) will be issued a call. The details do not need to be shared during the pastor's visits. General figures are adequate at this time.

Review any relevant denominational or regional compensation guidelines in preparation for developing your compensation package. They may address salary responsibility, components of an annual salary, a suggested base salary, benefits, and moving expenses. There may be allowances based on the size of the congregation, the job description, experience, and education.

If your denomination has compensation guidelines, review them and determine to what extent you will use them. Ask how much leeway you have in making your compensation package. If you have options, identify specific areas that need to be considered as your package is developed.

You might be totally on your own in creating and presenting your compensation package. Appendix F is an "Addendum to the Letter of Call," which presents a sample package. Identified in detail are times of work and hours, holidays and vacation, compensation, allowances, benefits, reimbursables, and additional agreements. You may feel this document is too specific, but it is much better to put things in writing than to debate later what is right or what is covered. Attention to details before the call can help prevent problems later. Your package does not have to be as detailed but should reflect standards for your area, benefits your church can afford, and allowances adequate for the pastor's profession. Individuals working on the compensation package should call neighboring churches to determine valid ranges. Use these as guidelines in determining dollar amounts appropriate for your church.

Once the basic compensation package is ready, several decisions need to be made. First, decide whether you need to make several specific packages based on the pastors who may be called. If you anticipate presenting two candidates, you may need one package for each pastor based on each pastor's experience and education level. Second, determine whether you will make allowances for negotiations in the terms of the package. There may be a request from the pastor to change the continuing education time or money, allow for a sabbatical after a certain number of years, or change other components.

The Issue of Pastoral Housing

Another area to discuss is pastoral housing. If the church owns a parsonage, state that fact in your church information packet. Of course, you hope the parsonage will meet the needs of the pastor's family. After they have seen the parsonage, sit down and discuss any improvements, whether as simple as painting and wallpapering or as complex as installing new carpet or upgrading a kitchen. Expecting the pastor to live in a substandard home, especially when compared to the rest of the congregation, is unrealistic.

If you have a small parsonage and the pastor has a large family, you will need to discuss your options. Will the church consider buying a larger parsonage or adding on to the existing one? Will you rent out the existing parsonage and purchase another one for the pastor? What you are able to do may influence a pastor's decision.

Many pastors find the option of owning a home to be attractive. This may hinge on whether he or she has built up equity from owning a home at a previous church. If the pastor will have the option of purchasing a home, let him or her know that you will find a reputable real estate agent. If the pastor has school-aged children, show the neighborhoods around the schools. If a home is to be purchased by the pastor, offer to help evaluate the local housing market. Whatever the option, do your best to help the pastor have everything ready before his or her family has to move. Having to rent for a short period, and then move again, is a hardship. If the pastor will live in the parsonage, consider providing an equity allowance.

If necessary, establish a task force to investigate the various options. Several possible arrangements are listed below. If you choose any arrangement other than the pastor living in the parsonage or the pastor buying a home without help from the congregation, be sure to have a lawyer or knowledgeable individual draw up an agreement that is fair to both parties. The housing market may change negatively or the pastor may leave sooner than expected, and the agreement protects involved parties. In all options, as in the examples below, clarify the responsibilities of each party, dates when payments are due, and conditions placed on either party.

- The pastor makes the down payment and all other payments and owns the house. The church pays the pastor a monthly housing allowance.
- Give the pastor a loan to apply to the down payment. This loan could be interest free or low interest for a time period, until another home is purchased, or until he or she leaves.
- Consider allowing the pastor to purchase the parsonage from the church.
- Create an equity share arrangement with the pastor and the church, with each putting in a predetermined amount and each having a percentage at risk.

In each of these instances, the pastor will still be paid a housing allowance, but is typically responsible for the maintenance, taxes, and insurance. Usually the pastor specifies what portion of his or her cash compensation will be designated as the housing allowance. The pastor has to be able to document for the Internal Revenue Service that the allowance was used for mortgage or rent, utilities, maintenance, furnishings, and other expenses. In an equity share arrangement, the church could be responsible for a percentage of any maintenance costs that exceed a predetermined amount agreed on by the pastor and the board. In all the options, the board needs to offer the pastor a fair housing allowance.

If you have a parsonage, work out the details of how maintenance will be managed. Is there an allotted amount of money for maintenance? Who is responsible for the work? What is the pastor responsible for? Who authorizes payments? If utilities are paid, determine which are covered: garbage, electricity, gas, telephone, and water. What about a pager, cell phone, or cable TV? While these may seem like simple questions, they can easily be overlooked and become problems later.

Presentation is everything. When pastors come to visit your church, they will watch closely how you present your church, its ministries, and the congregation. The congregation will be watching the pastors to see whether they are everything you said they were. A good presentation will help make the pastors' visits positive and exciting. Along with planning your presentation, you need to be working on how to manage the call process, the next step in the search process.

Task Cluster:
Presenting Your Best Side

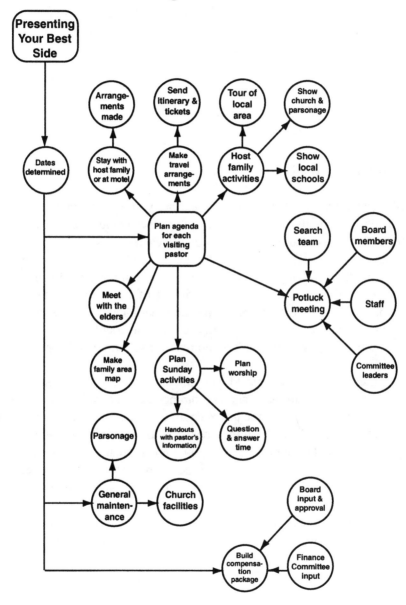

CHAPTER 10

Managing the Call Process

Guidelines for the Call Process

If your church belongs to a denomination, you need to know what your constitution and bylaws, church order, or other guidelines say about how the call process is to be done. The guidelines may be very basic and leave room for various forms of local church application or they may be very specific about rules you must follow. Do not move forward in the call process without a thorough understanding of the requirements of your guidelines. If you do not belong to a denomination with guidelines, you are free to proceed as the search committee and the board choose.

Guidelines typically address nominations, voting, and approval.

- Usually two people must be nominated for every open position.
- The search committee shall recommend one candidate to the board.
- The board is to seek the judgment of the congregation and consider it of significant weight in their decision to recommend a candidate.
- If the board concurs with the recommendation, the pastor is invited, as its pastoral choice, to lead worship and preach to the full congregation.
- The right to vote shall be limited to confessing members in good standing, as defined by the congregation.
- A two-thirds vote of the congregation is required to approve the pastor.
- The authority for making and carrying out final decisions remains with the board or the body designated by the congregation's constitution and bylaws.
- Upon approval from the regional office, the board may issue the formal call letter.

- When the call is accepted, the pastor's name is to be published on three successive Sundays so opportunity may be afforded to raise objections.

Options for the Call Process

Once the pastoral field has been narrowed down to the best three to five candidates, the search committee needs to consider what method it will use when deciding which pastor to call. Some search committees, with their board's support, may feel comfortable selecting one candidate to present to the congregation. Since the search committee theoretically knows more about the pastors and the congregation than anyone else, it is in the best position to judge the choices and recommend one pastor. Talk this over as a committee, and if you decide to recommend one pastor, present your case to the board and ask for its approval. If the board was expecting two candidates, be prepared to defend your selection of one candidate.

Other search committees will choose to present either two or three pastors, commonly called a duo or trio. It is easier to present two pastors than three. Two pastoral candidates can be invited to lead worship, preach, and meet with various groups, one after the other, on two consecutive Sundays. With two pastors, both Sunday worship services will remain fresh in people's minds. However, introducing three candidates over three Sundays makes it hard for people to remember which pastor they favor and for what reasons. Three candidates also tend to split the vote, making it more difficult to receive a wholehearted endorsement by the majority. Choosing between two pastors is hard enough without introducing a third pastor into the equation.

Once a slate of candidates has been chosen, you need to decide how to present the candidates and manage the voting process. Again, there are several options, all presented below as if two pastors were being introduced. Whatever the decision, the board is usually charged with overseeing the voting process.

- Present the candidates to the congregation. The congregation meets and votes. The board then affirms the congregation's decision.
- Present the candidates to the board. The board votes and the congregation is asked to affirm the board's decision.

- The search committee votes, the board affirms their work, and the congregation affirms the decisions of both the search committee and the board.

Designing Your Call Letter

Your letter of call should pertain to the work and proper support of the pastor. What are you calling the pastor to do? Is his or her role clearly defined? Is compensation a part of the letter? Guidelines often speak to how the letter of call is to be managed.

You have several options in making your letter of call. If your denomination has an official letter of call, review it to determine if it fits your needs and style. You may be required to use the official call letter, or it may be provided as a guide and you may be free to modify it. If you modify the letter, adhere to the basic intent. Any changes to the letter may have to be approved through your church supervisor or counselor.

The letter of call needs to be signed by the board or by whomever it designates. Depending on denominational protocol, it may also need to be signed by your church supervisor or counselor before being sent. Prepare the letter of call ahead of time and have it preapproved and signed by your supervisor or counselor. If you are presenting two pastors for a vote, prepare a call letter for each pastor in advance and have both letters signed by the supervisor or counselor. Either of these letters will then be ready to be sent as soon as the call is approved. Consider including a cover letter signed by members of the search committee.

At the end of this book are several documents that can be a part of your call package. Appendix E ("Letter of Call") defines the pastor's call. Appendix F ("Addendum to the Letter of Call") describes the compensation package. The letter of call and the addendum, together with Appendix D ("Cover Letter for the Letter of Call"), should all be signed by the full board and the full search committee. These documents will present a hospitable and quality pastoral call. Make your call package as personable as possible.

Determine if your denomination or regional offices have additional requirements affecting your issuing of a call letter. The supervisor or counselor may have to oversee the board vote, and the decision of your board may have to be presented to a regional board for final approval.

The Congregational Meeting

The congregational meeting to approve the call must be a formal business meeting. The recommendation from the search committee or board is presented, discussed, and put to a vote. Determine and publicize before the meeting who will be allowed to vote. Some denominations allow confessing members to vote, while others allow only active, confirmed members the voting privilege. Normally, only members are allowed the opportunity to vote.

Also determine and publicize what percentage of the congregation is required to vote for a candidate in order to call your next pastor. Some guidelines indicate that a call can be based on a simple majority, while others will require a two-thirds majority. Often, after a vote is taken, the board will ask for a unanimous vote from the congregation. Depending on your guidelines, the board may need to meet to approve the decision of the congregation. In some denominations the vote by the congregation is advisory to the board. There may be instances in which the board may choose not to issue the call that had been approved by the congregation. If this is this case, the board needs to meet with the search committee to clarify its decision and then inform the congregation, giving its rationale. In all cases, the congregation needs to be reminded of the need to determine the will of God for the church.

Celebrating the Call

An alternative to the formal congregational meeting is to call all members and friends of the congregation to make the decision within the context of worship. Come together to pray and worship with Scripture and song, announce the candidate, lead the congregation in small-group prayers, and then ask for a vote of affirmation. Close with praise songs and prayer. The sample service below (with songs italicized) can be modified to include your congregation's favorite songs and Scripture.

Congregational Prayer and Worship

Seek Ye First the Kingdom of God
Spirit Song
With All My Heart
Change My Heart, Oh Lord

Announcement of Candidate

Open My Eyes, Oh Lord

Prayer Sessions
   Opening Prayer
   Praise Prayers (Ps. 95:1-7)
   Confession Prayers (1 John 1:6 and Isa. 59:2)
   Thanksgiving Prayers (1 Chron. 16:8 and Ps. 105:5)
   Intercession Prayers (Phil. 4:6-7 and Luke 18:1)

Lord's Prayer
Surely the Presence
In Your Time

   Vote of Affirmation

Unto Thee, Oh Lord
Lord, Listen to Your Children Praying

   Closing Prayer

Once the decision is made, several things need to happen. First, the search committee chairperson should call the chosen pastor. Share the enthusiasm that the search committee, the board, and the congregation feel at this point. Explain that a formal letter of call will follow (preferably by overnight mail). Second, calls should be made to any other pastors considered. Third, call your church supervisor or counselor. Fourth, prepare the letter of call. Make two copies, one for your records and one to be sent to the pastor. The board secretary should retain a copy of the signed call letter for the church's minutes.

Generally, allow at least three weeks, or whatever is specified in the guidelines you are using, for a response. You might also talk with the pastor to settle on an appropriate length of time for him or her to make a decision. The pastor may request an extension. Keep in close contact through phone calls from the search committee chairperson and letters and cards from the search committee, board, staff, committee leaders, and the congregation. You do not want to be pushy, yet you want to be available to answer any questions. Phone calls from other search committee members, staff, or board members should be made only at the discretion of the search committee chairperson. Do not give the pastor's telephone number to the congregation. Respect the pastor's privacy and need for time to reflect, pray, and discuss the call with his or her family. Remember that some pastors may be considering two calls at one time, or may be at different stages of an inquiry process with other churches.

Prayer Vigils and Prayer Cards

From the start of the search process, the congregation has been praying. Now that they have chosen the pastor to be called, they need to be in focused prayer for the pastor. Make a poster on which members may sign up to pray in half-hour segments. They should pray for the pastor and his family and their decision. Place the poster in the foyer of the church and encourage people to sign up for a time period between 6:00A.M. to 10:00 P.M. Let the pastor know that the members are praying for him or her during this specific period. Members can also be encouraged to send cards and letters.

Another idea is for the search committee to make tent cards that fold in the middle and have the same text on both sides. Members may put these on their tables and on their desks at work. These prayer cards can be a helpful reminder to pray for the pastor and his or her family as they consider the call. A sample prayer card is included below.

Pray for Our Pastor of Call
Al Sayes

Pray for guidance
Pray for God's will for the Sayes family
Pray for Anytown Community Church

Al & Pat Sayes
Jamie (14), Jimmie (10), Jeffery (8)

Cards or letters may be sent to
8765 Lively Road
Orange, CA 53210

When the Answer Is Yes

When the pastor's response is positive, the happy news should be spread through the church membership quickly. Many have been in constant prayer for a positive response, and they must be informed of the decision. Celebrate with the congregation.

If your denomination has rules about how to inform the congregation of the acceptance, follow them. Some denominations require a posting of the new pastor's name for several weeks in case there are objections from the congregation. Hopefully you will not have such constraints, but if so, respect them.

The acceptance phone call may come to the president of the board or the chairperson of the search committee. Whoever receives the phone call needs to first telephone those who have dedicated themselves to constant prayer for the call. Then phone the members of the search committee and the board. The easiest method of getting the word out is to have the search committee, board members, or elders phone the members. Your supervisor or counselor should also be notified.

The positive response is an affirmation to the life and value of the congregation. Use the acceptance and its affirmation in the next worship service. If there is a letter from the pastor, read it before the congregation. Applaud God's work in your search efforts. Have a time of praise and prayer.

When the letter of acceptance comes, post it for the congregation to see. Encourage the congregation to send the pastor letters and cards that express their happiness. Maintain proactive communications until the pastor arrives. The church secretary should begin sending the new pastor copies of your weekly bulletin and the church newsletter. If the pastor has children, the Sunday school children or the youth group can make a video to say "Hi" to any children in their age group. The secretary of the board can send copies of the board minutes and committee reports so the new pastor will be aware of what is happening in the church's ministry structure. All of these communications help the pastor establish an identity with his or her future church home.

When the Answer Is No

For many months all of your energy was spent in the search process and then in issuing a call to your chosen pastor. Now you have received an answer, "No." As difficult as it may seem, you will need to pick up the pieces and regain the momentum you had before the call was declined.

Having the call declined will be hard for the search committee since you probably developed a close relationship with the candidate. Take time in your next meeting to talk about your feelings. Express your discouragement and then make a decision to move forward. Spend time in prayer. Even though you may be discouraged, remember to praise God and trust that the decision was God's will.

Handling Rejections

Rejection is hard to accept. One way of dealing with the negative response is to talk with the pastor and ask what factors influenced the decision to decline your call. Use the decline as an opportunity to learn. Is there something in your presentation that needs improving? Did the pastor pick up on underlying issues in the congregation that need to be resolved? Was there a sense that you really do not know who you are or where you are going as a congregation?

It is easy to take rejection personally, when in fact it is most likely due to simply not being a good match of the candidate's ministry gifts to your vision or the ministry strengths and weaknesses of your congregation. This perspective can help you maintain a proper focus.

Starting Over

In reality, you will not be starting from scratch. If you had presented two or three pastors to choose from, you will need to consider if any one of the other pastors will be your next choice. Do not automatically exclude them. One of these may be the right pastor. Some pastors will not entertain a call from a church that did not choose them first; others will. The committee needs to talk about it and decide whether to extend a call to one of them since you have already interviewed them, invited them out, and talked in depth with them. How did the congregation receive them? Was their worship style a good match? Dedicate yourselves to a time of prayer to this decision.

You also have your list of other pastors with whom you were working. Focus on this list. If you had pastors at the beginning stages of the process, work at bringing them further along in the process.

Some pastors who declined interest earlier may have indicated openness to hearing from you further down the road. Now may be the time. Call your regional or denominational offices and request more names. Talk to your contacts. Consider calling pastors who have seen your church packet, but who were not interested. Ask them about possible names to call or even if they might now be interested.

This is the time to stay focused. You have a wealth of information about other pastors with whom you have been working. And there are still pastors to discover. One of these is the pastor God has chosen for your church.

If you received a no, you will continue your search efforts. If you received a yes, it is time to begin planning for a smooth transition in leadership.

Task Cluster:
Managing the Call Process

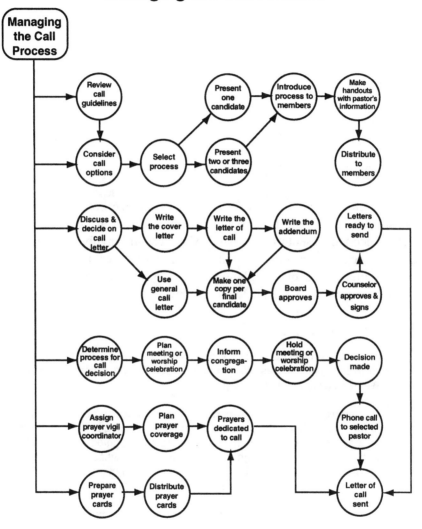

CHAPTER 11

Managing a Smooth Transition

Final Actions for the Search Committee

The search committee has a few details to finalize before it disbands. Outstanding bills need to be paid and a final report made to the board. Letters need to be sent to any pastors who were still involved in any stage of the search process, informing them of the acceptance. Be sure to return any audiotapes, videotapes, photographs, or other materials you received from these pastors. A sample letter is below.

Pastor Carol,

Our search process has ended. We thank you for being a part of it. It was with excitement this past week that we received an acceptance from Pastor Al Sayes to be our next pastor.

The search committee has a very warm spot in our hearts for you, for Tim, and for your ministry. We appreciate the honesty and genuineness that you conveyed in all our communications. As we struggled to find God's will for our church, we sought guidance in prayer. Although a call was issued to Pastor Al, we felt very positive about your potential for ministry and know that God has a special place for you with a congregation that will benefit from your warm and caring touch. It was a difficult decision for us to make. We feel that God led us to Pastor Al at this point in our congregation's life. We also feel God led us to you and want you to know how good we feel about you, and how we as a search committee would be honored to pray for you.

Our prayer for you is that you and your family will allow God to lead you into a new ministry or a recommitment in your current ministry that fully utilizes your gifts for ministry.

If we can assist you in any way, please let us know. We would be happy to provide a reference or perspective to another search committee regarding your ministry potential.

The search committee may decide to go out to dinner together to celebrate a positive conclusion to its efforts. Celebrate God's working in your search process.

The Role of the Board during the Transition

When the call is accepted and announced to the congregation, the search committee members will begin to phase themselves out of the picture. Technically, they have completed their job. Now the board needs to take over and manage the transition. The full board may choose to be involved or it may have the transition managed by a transition committee or an administration committee. A starting date needs to be determined, allowing appropriate time for the new pastor to close his or her current ministry and, if necessary, to relocate. Additionally, an installation date and service must be planned. Moving arrangements may need to be coordinated and housing arrangements made. Guest pastors need to be coordinated until the new pastor arrives.

The board needs to help the new pastor make the transition into the life of the board, staff, committees, the congregation, and the community. Ask the pastor and spouse if there is any information that would be helpful to them as they plan their move. Dinners can be planned and socials organized. Provide the names and telephone numbers of local area pastors in order to establish important contacts. Business cards and stationery need to be ordered. Make an area map which shows locations of all the church families, and provide a complete set of area maps. If the pastor is coming ahead of his or her family due to the children's school or spouse's job constraints, consider giving a shopping basket full of food. Check ahead about favorite foods. Keep in mind that your new pastor is still a pastor somewhere else. Be realistic about your expectations.

Continuation of the New Pastor's Benefits

Once the call is accepted, a start date will be determined between the new pastor and the appropriate members of the board. This date will be determined in part by the pastor's release date at the previous church. Children's school terms, a spouse's job constraints, the sale of their home, or a vacation between assignments may also affect the starting date.

The pastor's insurance and pension coverage can often be continued from the previous church. Be sure to ask if there are unusual circumstances that may require you to pick up the insurance or pension payments prior to the actual installation date. Although this may affect only a small number of pastors, there may be situations in which a pastor is paying for coverage or has had coverage terminated. The former church may have closed, or the pastor may have been on a sabbatical or on the mission field.

Credentials and Membership Papers

Depending on denominational protocol, the incoming pastor will make the necessary calls to have his or her credentials retained at the denominational office or released and sent to your church or a regional office, whichever is appropriate. If the papers are sent to a regional office, request a copy for your board. The pastor will normally also take steps to have the membership papers of his or her family transferred to your church.

Determine whether the secretary of the board or the pastor will notify the necessary regional or denominational offices of the ministry change and starting date, or follow whatever procedures are in place for your denomination.

The Installation Service

The board or the elders, the incoming pastor, and the worship leader (if different from the pastor), need to plan the installation service. Local pastors and members of their churches may be invited. You may choose to have a special service with a guest pastor, special praise team or choir numbers, special member involvement, and the laying on of hands by other pastors or the board. The service will be the starting point of the life of the pastor and your congregation. Make this a service of celebration. It needs to be an especially meaningful service for the pastor, his or her family, and the church. Some congregations have a reception or meal after the service.

If there are regional or denominational guidelines for an installation service, respect them. If this is the case, members from your church, the new pastor, and the supervisor or counsel, or other regional representatives might meet to plan the service.

Retaining Information for the Next Search Committee

Once the search committee has been disbanded, several things need to happen. All pastoral profile forms should first be destroyed. The search committee secretary or chairperson should then assemble one set of materials for record purposes. This set of materials, minus the pastoral profiles, should be stored in a secure location at the church and be available only to those with a need to know. The material will be helpful down the road when another search committee must be formed. (One of the difficulties of forming an effective search committee is that since a search is not done regularly, it is often hard to find people who have served before. Retaining this material can be helpful to the chairperson of the next search committee.) Committee members need to properly dispose of their search materials and related papers and notes.

Once again, as a group, celebrate God's direction for your church. Many individuals have been blessed by their service on a pastoral search committee. You may be blessed with spiritual growth, a new awareness of the power of prayer, an understanding of your church and its members and ministries, and a personal closeness to your new pastor. Celebrate God's gifts to the search committee and the gift of a new pastor for your church.

Task Cluster:
Managing a Smooth Transition

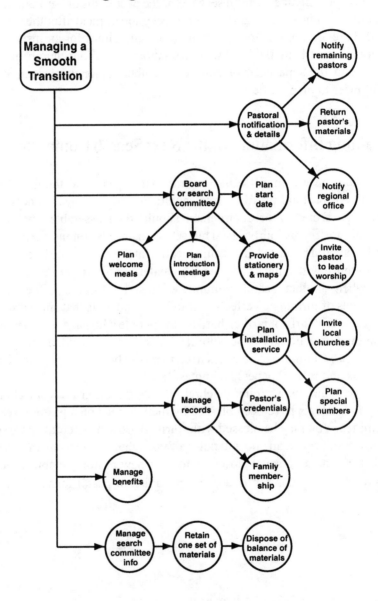

Congregational Survey

Anytown Community Church
Congregational Survey

Information from this survey will be used to aid the Pastoral Search Committee in the process of selecting a pastor. It will assist in the evaluation of our unique needs as a congregation as well as allow prospective pastors an insight into who we are. Because the search committee is trying to move quickly to develop a profile of our church, <u>we ask that these surveys be returned by the evening of August 14</u>. Please place completed surveys in the box on the table in the foyer or mail them to the church. We may not be able to incorporate into the church profile any surveys returned at a later date.

We ask that each regularly attending teenager and adult complete a survey. Completed results will be posted. Individual responses are confidential. Your input is extremely important, and we thank you for your participation.

Name: _____

Anytown Community Church Affiliation Information

Please circle your answer.

Anytown Community Church affiliation: Member   Nonmember

Length of time associated with Anytown Community Church:
less than 1 year   1-5 years   6-10 years   11-20 years   over 20 years

Personal Information

Please circle your answer.

Please indicate your sex: Male   Female

Please indicate your age range:
13-19   20-29   30-39   40-49   50-59   60-69   70 and over

Please indicate your occupational category:
Student   Homemaker   Professional   Trades   Sales   Agriculture
Business   Retired   Other _____

Please indicate your ethnic background:
Caucasian   African American   Hispanic   Asian
Native American   Other _____

Other than Sunday worship, do you participate in any ministries, programs, or activities of the church?
Yes   No

Do you participate in any outreach (i.e., evangelistic) ministries?
Yes   No

Desired Professional Qualities of Our Next Pastor

Circle one for each topic:
1 = unimportant, 2 = important, 3 = very important

Preaching	1 2 3	Ministering to families	1 2 3
Conducting worship	1 2 3	Church administration	1 2 3
Teaching	1 2 3	Ministering to the sick	1 2 3
Pastoral care	1 2 3	Conflict resolution	1 2 3
Counseling	1 2 3	Community involvement	1 2 3
Problem solving	1 2 3	Cooperation with the boards	1 2 3
Program development	1 2 3	Setting vision and goals	1 2 3
Evangelism leadership	1 2 3	Youth and children	1 2 3
Ministering to elderly	1 2 3	Training others for leadership	1 2 3
Ministering to youth	1 2 3	Building committees	1 2 3

Our Expectations for the New Pastor

Rank the following list in numeric order with 1 being the most important and 8 being the least important.

Makes it a priority to visit the church members _____
Is energetic and charismatic in worship _____
Makes the worship service his or her main focus _____
Works with the board in setting visionary leadership _____
Helps us develop a strong outreach into the community _____
Helps us develop small groups _____
Develops strong board and committee leadership _____
Helps us develop more programs for members and visitors _____

Strengths, Weaknesses, and Needs of Our Congregation

Please evaluate the relative strength of our church in these ministry areas.
Circle one for each topic: 1 = weakness, 2 = average, 3 = strength

Evangelism	1 2 3	Discipleship	1 2 3
Community outreach	1 2 3	Global mission support	1 2 3
Doctrinal teaching	1 2 3	Managing conflict	1 2 3

Ministry to children	1	2	3	Ministry to youth	1	2	3
Ministry to singles	1	2	3	Ministry to families	1	2	3
Ministry to elderly	1	2	3	Ministry to women	1	2	3
Ministry to men	1	2	3	Ministry to seniors	1	2	3
Bible studies	1	2	3	Spiritual growth	1	2	3
Fellowship	1	2	3	Caring for the poor	1	2	3
Music ministry	1	2	3	Making visitors			
Liturgy	1	2	3	feel welcome	1	2	3
Unity	1	2	3	Worship services	1	2	3
Shepherding	1	2	3	Caregiving	1	2	3
Nurturing	1	2	3	Faithfulness	1	2	3
Commitment	1	2	3	Counseling services	1	2	3
Denominational				Stewardship	1	2	3
participation	1	2	3	Supporting families	1	2	3
Adult education	1	2	3	Sunday school	1	2	3
Administration	1	2	3	Vacation Bible school	1	2	3
Openness to change	1	2	3	Being goal-orientated	1	2	3
Cooperation with				Defining our mission			
other churches	1	2	3	and vision statements	1	2	3

Congregational Interests

Circle one for each sentence:
1 = false, 2 = somewhat true, 3 = true

Our members care about each other.	1	2	3
Our members volunteer readily for church activities.	1	2	3
Our members give generous financial support to the church.	1	2	3
Our congregation supports its committees.	1	2	3
Members with broken lives find a safe haven in our church.	1	2	3
Our congregation supports the board.	1	2	3
The board encourages the use of members' talents in the worship services.	1	2	3
The board sets worthy examples for the congregation.	1	2	3
Our congregation cooperated well with our previous pastor.	1	2	3
Our next pastor can count on the wholehearted cooperation of the congregation.	1	2	3

Please contact a member of the search committee if you have any
questions regarding this questionnaire.

Pastoral Questionnaire

Please write a few thoughts about each topic listed below. We are interested, for your sake and ours, in relevant and concise statements of your thoughts and feelings as these phrases relate to you and your ministry.

Personal Information

Name _____

Age _____   Years Pastoring _____
Home Phone (___)_____   Office Phone (___)_____
E-mail _____
Fax   (___) _____

Spiritual gifts:
1) _____
2) _____
3) _____

My most challenging ministry areas are:

My most satisfying ministry areas are:

My growth areas are:

Why do you want to change churches?

What is missing in your current church that you would like to find with us?

Spouse's name _____

Does your spouse have a role in your ministry or in the church?
If so, please describe.

Children:

1)_____age ___   2)_____age ___

3)_____age ___   4)_____age ___

5)_____age ___

Do you own your own home?   yes _____ no _____

Would you prefer to live in a parsonage _____ or your own home ____?

Your Thoughts about Leadership

My style of leadership is:

My relationship to the board will be:

My relationship to staff and committee leaders will be:

Developing and nurturing a vision means:

Involving others in lay ministry means:

I mentor others by:

I foster commitment and accountability by:

Your Thoughts about Administration

Administration of the church should be:

The board and committees assist in church's administration by:

Your Thoughts about Worship

The worship style I prefer is:

My preaching and teaching styles are:

Lay participation should include:

I think formal and informal worship are:

Your Thoughts about Education

Good children and youth programs include:

Family ministry means:

Adult education should be:

Your Thoughts about Evangelism

Evangelism allows the church to:

Training others for evangelism means:

Evangelism should be:

Your Thoughts about Fellowship

Good church fellowship is:

I think family visiting is:

Caring for each other means:

Questions you might have of us?
Please write any questions you may have on another piece of paper.

Introducing Two Candidates to the Congregation

Anytown Community Church
Pastoral Search Committee

Dear Members and Friends of Anytown Community Church,

The Pastoral Search Committee requests and encourages full participation of the congregation in the next phase of the pastoral search process.

Prior to inviting pastoral candidates to Anytown Community Church to meet the congregation, each prospective candidate provided considerable written, oral, and recorded correspondence. The search committee has made every effort to identify ministry style and personality characteristics in an attempt to match the skills and gifts of the prospective candidate with the unique qualities and needs of Anytown Community Church.

We present two candidates at this time, believing fully that both are well suited and qualified for ministry with us. Attached are profiles of Al Sayes who will be here on January 10, and Carol Collins who will be here on January 17. Please review their profiles prior to their visits.

During the upcoming visits, the pastors and their spouses will have an opportunity to meet with the board, staff, and committee leaders. They will also tour the community and other points of interest. On Sunday the visiting pastor will lead us in our morning worship. After worship there will be a question and answer time for the congregation to interact directly with the candidate. A fellowship time will follow.

After both candidates have completed their visits, each member and friend of the congregation will have an opportunity to evaluate the candidates and indicate which one is best suited for ministry here.

The information gained from this process, in addition to the prior research, will be considered by the search committee in determining which candidate to recommend to the board for a call. If the board endorses the candidate, the recommendation will be presented to the congregation for a vote of affirmation. A Congregational Prayer and Worship celebration is scheduled for Sunday evening, January 17 at 6:30 P.M. for this vote.

In the event that a candidate receives our call but declines to accept it, the search committee may recommend the other candidate for a call, provided he or she meets the acceptability criteria set by the search committee.

During this phase of the process we again ask for your fervent prayers for each of the candidates and the search committee as well, that we all will be receptive to the leading of the Holy Spirit. For ultimately, we acknowledge that it is God who calls the man or woman, and God merely uses us as willing servants to accomplish this task.

If you have questions about the candidates or the process, please call any member of the search committee.

Cover Letter for the Letter of Call

Pastor Al,

It is with great excitement and anticipation that we sign this cover letter to our letter of call. We invite you to minister with us and to us in the Lord's work at Anytown Community Church.

You have touched our hearts, given warmth, and provided a sense of hope into what we can do together as God's church ministering to each other and wanting to minister more to our community. We believe that your gifts, ministry style, leadership skills, and personality style can move us towards our vision and mission while keeping us focused on our core values.

We believe we can offer you a church family who will love you and care for you and your family personally. We commit to work side by side with you in the Lord's work, to serve under your leadership, and to be happy in the Lord with you.

The attached letter of call has been committed to the Lord. We trust in the Lord's guidance as you consider this call to ministry here with us. Our prayers will be with you and your family as you commit this decision to the Lord.

With God's love and in his service,

Board Members   Pastoral Search
                                 Committee Members

_____   _____

_____   _____

_____   _____

Letter of Call

Anytown Community Church
Letter of Call

Dear Pastor Al,

The Board of Anytown Community Church has the honor and pleasure to inform you that you have been chosen by a unanimous vote at a congregational meeting held on the 17th day of January 1999, to be our minister of the Word.

On behalf of our congregation, we therefore extend to you this letter of call and pray that you will come and minister to us and with us.

The work that we expect of you, should it please the Lord to send you to us, consists of preaching and teaching, leadership of the church and the board, family visiting and calling on the sick with the help of the elders, and all things that pertain to the work of a faithful and diligent servant of the Lord, all in accord with the Word of God. The attached paper, "Pastoral Responsibilities and Relationships," further defines these areas.

We know that the laborer is worthy of his [or her] hire. To encourage you in the discharge of your duties and to free you from material need while you are ministering God's Word to us, the board of Anytown Community Church promises to pay you a positive compensation package, allowances for benefits, and reimbursables to offset expenses. These amounts are detailed in the addendum to this letter of call.

May the King of the church impress this call upon your heart and give you guidance that you may arrive at a decision that is pleasing to him and, if possible, gratifying to us.

Yours in Christ,

The Board of Anytown Community Church of Anytown, Massachusetts

Done this 17th day of January 1999.

_____, President of the Board

_____, Secretary

_____, Church Counselor

Addendum to the Letter of Call

An Addendum to the Letter of Call between
the Board of the Anytown Community Church and Pastor Al Sayes

Times of Work and Leave

1) Your work includes not only activities directed to the Anytown Community Church and its well-being, but may also include work in the community on behalf of the church. The pastor's scheduled workweek is five days, which shall include Sunday activities. The pastor is expected to preserve at least one 24-hour period each week solely for personal and family time.

2) You will have the following periods of leave at full compensation:
    a) _____ national holidays and _____ floating holidays to be taken so as not to interfere with worship for the major church seasons.
    b) _____ weeks of annual vacation consisting of _____ workdays which shall include _____ Sundays. No more than _____ days and _____ Sundays may be carried over into the following year unless agreed upon in mutual consent with the board.
    c) _____ days of continuing education leave are granted each year, with _____ Sundays off.

Compensation

1) Your annual base salary will be _____. This salary, along with the allowances, benefits, and reimbursables listed below, will be paid monthly.

2) Your annual compensation, allowances, benefits, and reimbursables package will be reviewed and adjusted annually.

Allowances

The church shall pay the following allowances:
1) A Social Security offset allowance of _____.
2) The use of the parsonage, or a housing allowance in the amount of _____ annually.

Benefits

The church shall pay the following benefits:
1) Medical and dental insurance in the amount of _____ to provide full family coverage.
2) Pastor's life insurance.
3) Pension contribution.
4) A Christian school tuition fund in the amount of _____ for tuition assistance for any elementary school, high school, or full-time, four-year college dependent(s).
5) Parsonage utilities (except personal, long-distance calls).

Reimbursables

The church shall pay the following reimbursables as incurred in fulfilling the duties of your office:
1) Travel expenses, up to _____ yearly, will be paid monthly at the mileage rate established by the Internal Revenue Service and will include out-of-pocket costs for parking fees and tolls.
2) Hospitality expenses, up to _____ yearly, will be reimbursed monthly for expenses incurred in the course of professional and social activities on behalf of Anytown Community Church.
3) Books, magazines, and other related professional materials expenses will be reimbursed monthly, up to _____ yearly, for materials necessary to maintain the pastor's library and resources.
4) Expenses for continuing education, up to _____ yearly, shall be

reimbursed monthly. Upon mutual agreement, for specific continued education, ____ percent of this amount may be carried over to the next year.

Roles, Responsibilities, Relationships, and Support

1) The pastoral responsibilities and relationships are described in the paper following this addendum. Described are areas of leadership, authority, commitment, vision casting, personal giftedness, equipping and enabling, and relationships to staff, board members, and committee leaders.
2) The Pastoral Relations Committee functions to aid in your spiritual and emotional well-being.

Other Agreements

1) If you are of a mind to purchase a home, and finances of both parties allow, the board will negotiate with you for an acceptable housing allowance or equity share agreement.
2) All moving and travel expenses incurred in making your move to the Anytown area will be paid by the Anytown Community Church.
3) All pay and benefits shall become effective on a mutually agreed-upon date.
4) All compensation, allowances, benefits, reimbursables, vacation, and continuing education leave will be prorated for any partial years of service.
5) The letter of call and this addendum shall be made part of the minutes of the next Anytown Community Church board meeting following its signing by both parties.

_____January 17, 1999_____   _____
Date   President of the Board

                                                           _____
                                                            Secretary
Concurrence:

_____   _____
Date   Pastor

Pastoral Responsibilities and Relationships

Leadership

The pastor, with the elders, is to provide spiritual leadership of the Church. The pastor is first called to a ministry of preaching and teaching of the Word, and second, to the equipping of the saints. Leadership in other areas must be based upon personal giftedness. Realizing that everything rises and falls on leadership, the ministry of leadership must be a key priority of the pastor. Leadership through influence must be built on trust and respect.

Authority

The pastor has the authority given by Scripture, which defines his or her office and ministry. He or she is to be supported by the board, staff, and committee leaders. As the spiritual leader of the congregation, the pastor shall work through the board to direct and lead. The Pastoral Relations Committee will address problems with authority. Certain responsibilities and authorities have been delegated by the board to committees as defined in our *Policy and Structure Manual*; therefore, that organizational structure must be respected and utilized to the best extent possible.

Commitment

The pastor must be committed to the vision and mission statements of Anytown Community Church and the ministries that flow from them. This commitment will be reflected in the pastor's service to the board and committees, the church membership, prayer, the ministries of Anytown Community Church, and the pastor's continuing pastoral education.

Vision Development

The pastor shall set the vision for the church, through the Administration Committee, and in cooperation with the board. The pastor's giftedness and position allow sharper insight and a broader view than others. The pastor needs to allow board members their visions, and the board needs to allow the pastor his or her vision. Collectively, a single vision statement is to be developed. Supporting goals and objectives need to be developed or refined annually. These then need to be presented before the congregation for its support.

Personal Giftedness

Recognizing that each individual is uniquely gifted for ministry, the pastor may choose to delegate certain areas of his or her service to others, or assume areas of service not previously taken. The Pastoral Relations Committee should affirm the pastor's ministries. Staff and committee leaders can also provide input. Reviews of the pastor's ministry areas should be done annually in conjunction with the pastoral evaluation.

Equipping and Enabling

The pastor shall minister to and mentor key leaders and potential leaders within the church body. This may be done through teaching in specific areas such as gifts, administration, discipleship, prayer, and vision development, and may include attending seminars with board members or key leaders. This time spent equipping and enabling leaders should be a ministry priority. Equipping and enabling of the general congregation should be done through sermons and Sunday school teaching.

Relationship to Staff

The pastor is ordinarily charged with the supervision of the staff. This may be changed by the individual job descriptions if supported by the Pastoral Relations Committee. The hiring and termination of staff will be in accordance with their individual contracts and should be reviewed by the Pastoral Relations Committee.

Relationship to Board

The pastor is ordinarily the president of board. Mutual and responsible leadership is expected from both the pastor and board members. Each has the authority to hold the other accountable. Mutual submission is necessary. Likewise, mutual submission to the will, wisdom, and vision of God for the church–at this time, in this place, and with God's people–is vital. Just as the board is to do an annual pastoral evaluation, so the pastor should do an annual board evaluation. The Pastoral Relations Committee will address problem areas as necessary.

Relationship to Committee Leaders

The pastor shall work closely with the committee leaders. The pastor, with the help of the Administration Committee, is responsible for equipping and managing the committee leaders to serve more effectively in their ministry roles.

BIBLIOGRAPHY

Achtemeier, Elizabeth. *So You're Looking for a New Preacher: A Guide for Pulpit Nominating Committees*. Grand Rapids: Wm. B. Eerdmans Publishing Co., 1991.

Berkley, James D., ed. "Negotiating the Terms of a Call" and "Calling Ministerial and Program Staff." In *Leadership and Administration*. Vol. 3 of *Leadership Handbooks of Practical Theology*. Grand Rapids: Baker Books, 1994.

Biehl, Bobb. *Pastoral Search Process*. Laguna Niguel, Calif.: Masterplanning Group International, 1991.

Ketcham, Bunty, and Celia Hahn. *So You're on the Search Committee*. Washington, D.C.: The Alban Institute, 1985.

Mead, Loren B. *Critical Moment of Ministry: A Change of Pastors*. Washington, D.C.: The Alban Institute, 1986.

Virkler, Henry A. *Choosing a New Pastor: The Complete Handbook*. Nashville: Oliver-Nelson Books, 1992.